SPMG

SHM
Scottish Heinemann Maths

5

Textbook

Heinemann

Heinemann is an imprint of Pearson Education Limited, a company incorporate in England
and Wales, having its registered office at Edinburgh Gate, Harlow, Essex, CM20 2JE.
Registered company number 872828

Heinemann is a registered trademark of Pearson Education Ltd

Writing team
John T Blair
Percy W Farren
Myra A Pearson
John W Thayers
David K Thomson

First Published 2002

11
10 9

ISBN 978 0 435177 66 9

Typeset and layout by Mandy Emery.
Illustrated by Debbie Clark, David Till, David Kearney, Jon Mitchell,
Derek Brazell, Diane Fawcett and Tony O'Donnell.
Cover Illustation by Gary Dunn.
Printed in Malaysia, CTP KHL

Contents

1 (a) Jamie has 2170 stamps.
He buys 10 more.
How many stamps has Jamie now?

(b) Polly has 1880 stamps.
She buys 100 more.
How many stamps has Polly now?

2 (a) 10 more than 6000

(b) 10 more than 5496

(c) 10 less than 2562

(d) 10 less than 3400

(e) 100 more than 9900

(f) 100 more than 4732

(g) 100 less than 6123

(h) 100 less than 10 000

(i) 50 more than 9700

(j) 50 more than 1950

(k) 50 less than 4000

(l) 50 less than 8300

3 Alan 7040 ALBUM   Benjy 5995 STAMPS   Cara 3650 ALBUM   Daljit 7990 ALBUM   Emma 8000   Faye 10 000

How many stamps does each person have after
(a) Alan gives Benjy 100 stamps   (b) Cara gives Emma 50 stamps
(c) Faye gives Daljit 10 stamps?

4 Write the multiples of 10 between
(a) 3210 and 3250   (b) 6480 and 6520   (c) 8015 and 7975

5 Write **a** multiple of 100 between
(a) 2500 and 2100   (b) 7806 and 8206   (c) 10 000 and 9600

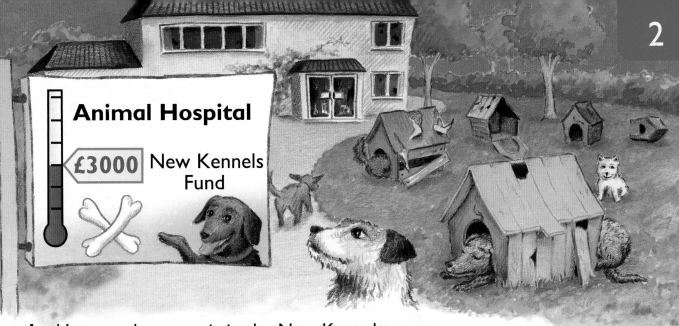

Animal Hospital

£3000 New Kennels Fund

1   How much money is in the New Kennels Fund after it is given **£1000 more?**

2   Write each amount.
(a) £1000 more   (b) £1000 more   (c) £1000 less   (d) £1000 less

 £6400    £900   £5050   £1700

(e) £500 more   (f) £500 less   (g) £500 more   (h) £500 less

 £8000   £4500    £9500   £6002

(i) £1000 more   (j) £1000 less   (k) £1000 more   (l) £1000 less

 £8175   £7638   £2523   £1809

3   Write the multiple of 1000
(a) after 2000   (b) before 8731.

4   Which multiple of 1000 is between
(a) 4000 and 6000   (b) 7294 and 6294?

3

1 What is the value of the **2** in each number?

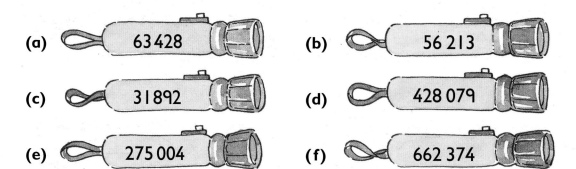

(a) 63 428

(b) 56 213

(c) 31 892

(d) 428 079

(e) 275 004

(f) 662 374

2 What is the value of the red digit in each number?

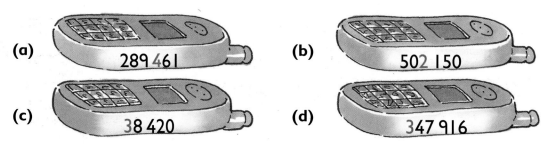

(a) 289 461

(b) 502 150

(c) 38 420

(d) 347 916

3

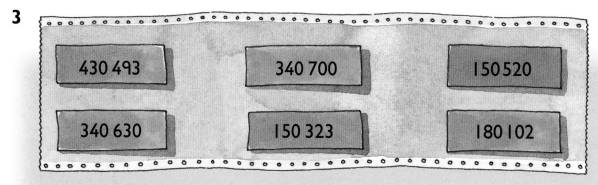

430 493   340 700   150 520

340 630   150 323   180 102

Which number
(a) has 340 thousands and an even hundreds digit
(b) is less than 2 hundred thousands and has tens digit 0
(c) has 150 thousands and 3 units
(d) has 340 thousands and fewer than 7 hundreds?

4 Use the digits $\boxed{3}$ $\boxed{4}$ $\boxed{6}$ $\boxed{7}$ $\boxed{9}$ to make a number which

(a) is greater than fifty thousand
(b) has a tens digit double the units digit
(c) has a hundreds digit equal to the sum of the units and tens digits.

I Write the larger number.

(a) 306 545   306 554   (b) 745 800   745 900

2 Write the smaller number.

(a) 699 350   681 710   (b) 149 999   159 100

3 Which number is   **(a)** largest   **(b)** smallest?

640 600   930 334   634 607

930 434   640 700   930 443

4 List in order.

(a) Start with the largest.

143 850   314 580   548 310   341 085   538 140

(b) Start with the smallest.

649 200   600 310   648 350   640 990   600 250

5 Write True (T) **or** False (F).

(a) $74500 < 75400$ (b) $650000 > 560000$

6 Complete using > or <.

(a) 135000 ▇ 235000   (b) 398000 ▇ 389000

(c) 787780 ▇ 787807   (d) 342600 ▇ 346200

1 Write the clipboard numbers so that they are **all** correct.

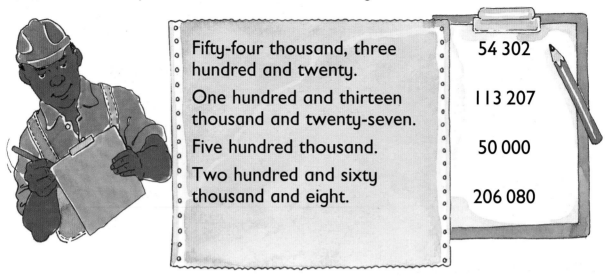

Fifty-four thousand, three hundred and twenty.	54 302
One hundred and thirteen thousand and twenty-seven.	113 207
Five hundred thousand.	50 000
Two hundred and sixty thousand and eight.	206 080

2 Write each number using **numerals**.

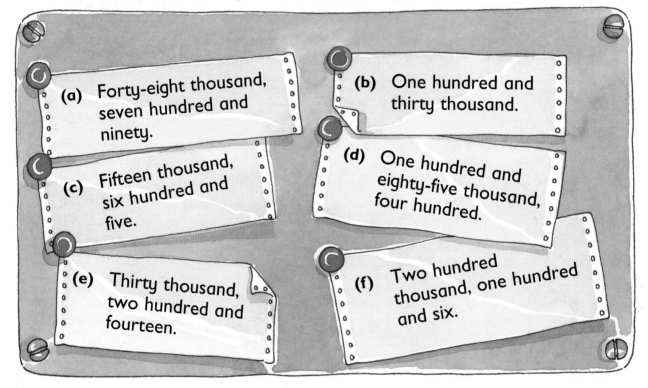

(a) Forty-eight thousand, seven hundred and ninety.

(b) One hundred and thirty thousand.

(c) Fifteen thousand, six hundred and five.

(d) One hundred and eighty-five thousand, four hundred.

(e) Thirty thousand, two hundred and fourteen.

(f) Two hundred thousand, one hundred and six.

3 Write **in words**.

(a) 24 000   (b) 640 000   (c) 73 800
(d) 102 650   (e) 400 000   (f) 102 036

1 Medals were given to the first hundred runners to complete a Fun Run.

What colour is the medal for

(**a**) thirty-fourth   (**b**) fifty-seventh   (**c**) sixty-second

(**d**) eighty-first   (**e**) ninety-sixth   (**f**) seventy-fifth?

2 Write each person's position.

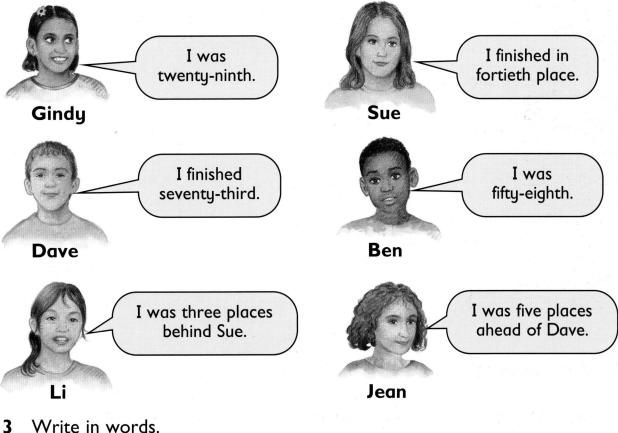

Gindy — I was twenty-ninth.

Sue — I finished in fortieth place.

Dave — I finished seventy-third.

Ben — I was fifty-eighth.

Li — I was three places behind Sue.

Jean — I was five places ahead of Dave.

3 Write in words.

(**a**) 35th   (**b**) 27th   (**c**) 52nd   (**d**) 99th

1 Estimate. About how many kilometres

* has each tanker travelled

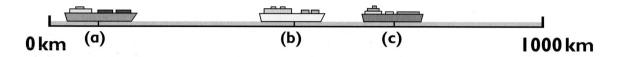

0 km   (a)   (b)   (c)   1000 km

* has each yacht travelled

0 km   (d)   (e)   (f)   50 km

* has each fishing boat travelled?

0 km   (g)   (h)   (i)   200 km

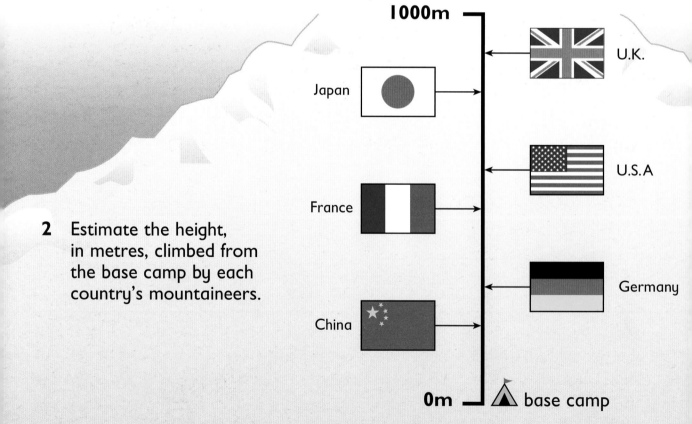

2 Estimate the height, in metres, climbed from the base camp by each country's mountaineers.

1000m — U.K.

Japan

U.S.A

France

Germany

China

0m — base camp

1 Write each price to the **nearest hundred** pounds.

(a) Computer

£845

(b) CD system

£405

(c) Camcorder

£777

(d) £91   (e) £450   (f) £969

2 Write each price to the **nearest ten** pounds.

(a) DVD player

£212

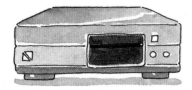

(b) Television

£994

(c) Microwave

£146

(d) £303   (e) £628   (f) £195

3 Write the price of each of these items

- to the nearest hundred pounds **and**
- to the nearest ten pounds.

(a) Mountain bike £249   (b) Washing machine £557

(c) Antique vase £185   (d) Digital camera £223

(e) Gold watch £651   (f) Football season ticket £318

(g) Aeroplane ticket to Australia £472

(h) Designer clothes outfit £399

1 List the numbers

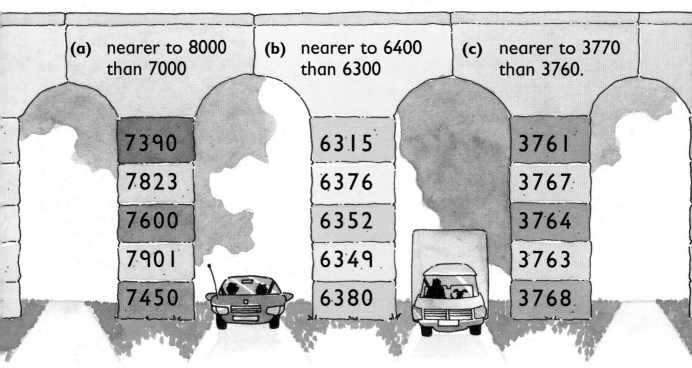

(a) nearer to 8000 than 7000	(b) nearer to 6400 than 6300	(c) nearer to 3770 than 3760.
7390	6315	3761
7823	6376	3767
7600	6352	3764
7901	6349	3763
7450	6380	3768

2 Write

• to the nearest thousand

(a) 5055   (b) 3333   (c) 736   (d) 9500

• to the nearest hundred

(e) 4281   (f) 8050   (g) 2111   (h) 1042

• to the nearest ten

(i) 9012   (j) 4784   (k) 3625   (l) 3996

3 Write the number of miles each car has travelled

(a) to the nearest thousand

(b) to the nearest hundred

(c) to the nearest ten.

| 7 8 3 6 |
| 4 2 5 1 |
| 9 7 0 9 |
| 2 3 6 5 |

1 Double each number.

(a) 61
(b) 74
(c) 83
(d) 54
(e) 92
(f) 94
(g) 53
(h) 72
(i) 81

2 Write each number on a **red** ticket with its double on a **yellow** ticket.

58 77 86
99 65 56

112 130 198
172 154 116

3

(a) Double 57
(b) Double 89
(c) Double 66
(d) 96 + 96
(e) 67 + 67
(f) 59 + 59

4

(a) 63 + 64
(b) 83 + 82
(c) 55 + 56
(d) 71 + 72
(e) 88 + 87
(f) 98 + 99
(g) 76 + 75
(h) 68 + 69
(i) 63 + 65
(j) 75 + 77
(k) 87 + 89
(l) 96 + 98

1 Write each number on a box with its double on a label.

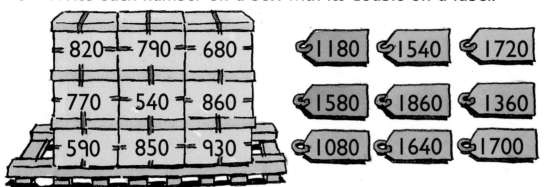

820   790   680

770   540   860

590   850   930

1180   1540   1720

1580   1860   1360

1080   1640   1700

2 Double each number.

(a) 740

(b) 5600

(c) 4900

(d) 8800

(e) 990

(f) 9500

(g) 1700

(h) 5700

(i) 2600

3

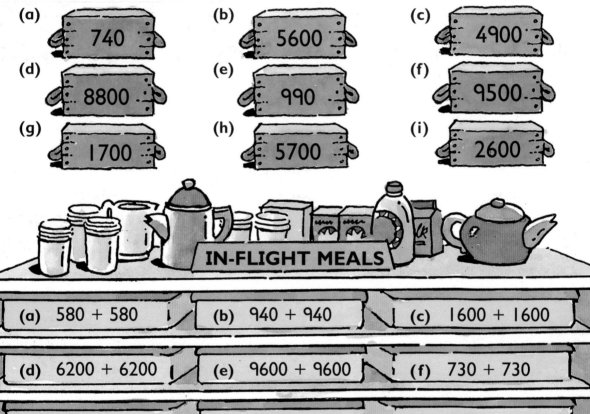

IN-FLIGHT MEALS

(a) 580 + 580

(b) 940 + 940

(c) 1600 + 1600

(d) 6200 + 6200

(e) 9600 + 9600

(f) 730 + 730

(g) 8400 + 8400

(h) 380 + 380

(i) 4200 + 4200

(j) 7600 + 7600

(k) 5300 + 5300

(l) 660 + 660

(m) 920 + 920

(n) 1900 + 1900

(o) 3700 + 3700

4 Which number when doubled gives

(a) 1020   (b) 1600   (c) 14 200   (d) 15 000?

1 What is the total weight of each set of packages.

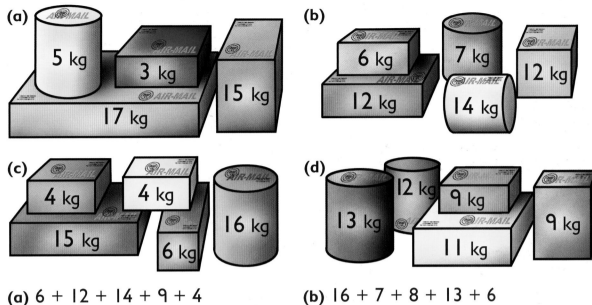

(a)
5 kg
3 kg
15 kg
17 kg

(b)
6 kg
7 kg
12 kg
12 kg
14 kg

(c)
4 kg
4 kg
16 kg
15 kg
6 kg

(d)
12 kg
9 kg
13 kg
11 kg
9 kg

2 (a) 6 + 12 + 14 + 9 + 4   (b) 16 + 7 + 8 + 13 + 6
   (c) 5 + 9 + 11 + 9 + 15   (d) 17 + 4 + 9 + 17 + 16

3 Find the total volume in each set of tanks.

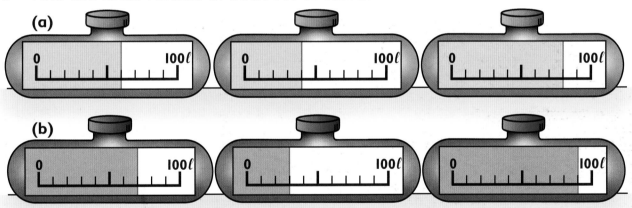

(a)
0   100 l
0   100 l
0   100 l

(b)
0   100 l
0   100 l
0   100 l

4 (a) 40 + 70 + 80   (b) 70 + 60 + 40   (c) 50 + 30 + 70   (d) 90 + 40 + 20

5 Find the total number of passengers carried by each airport taxi.

Driver	Fri	Sat	Sun
Tom	24	32	16
Ahmed	33	27	17
Gail	27	36	13

Driver	Fri	Sat	Sun
Debbie	34	26	14
Pete	21	29	19
Scott	15	33	26

Fruit 'n' Juice

1 **Fruit drinks sold on Saturday.**

 272   50   197   70

 60   90   286   365

Find the total number sold of:

(a) and   **(b)** and   **(c)** and

(d)  and    **(e)** and    **(f)**  and

2 **(a)** $347 + \blacksquare = 417$ **(b)** $\blacksquare + 60 = 235$ **(c)** $474 + \blacksquare = 504$

3 **Fruit sold in July.**

278 apples	31 melons	374 oranges	49 pineapples
194 bananas	59 limes	293 lemons	41 pears

Find the total number sold of:

(a) apples and pineapples   **(b)** oranges and limes
(c) pears and bananas   **(d)** lemons and melons
(e) apples and pears   **(f)** pineapples and bananas.

4 **(a)** $284 + 29$ **(b)** $363 + 61$ **(c)** $192 + 21$
  (d) $358 + 59$ **(e)** $177 + 41$ **(f)** $485 + 39$
  (g) $156 + 72$ **(h)** $434 + 88$ **(i)** $276 + 52$

5 **(a)** $185 + \blacksquare = 216$ **(b)** $267 + \blacksquare = 316$ **(c)** $533 + \blacksquare = 614$
  (d) $\blacksquare + 39 = 223$ **(e)** $\blacksquare + 21 = 217$ **(f)** $\blacksquare + 69 = 547$

Addition: a three-digit number and a multiple/near multiple of 10, with bridging   **HOME ACTIVITY 4**

1 Paulo's Pizza Parlour opened last month.
   In the first week Paulo's takings were:

Mon	Tue	Wed	Thu	Fri	Sat	Sun
£241	£351	£400	£562	£723	£832	£613

In the second week Paulo's takings **increased** by:

Mon	Tue	Wed	Thu	Fri	Sat	Sun
£33	£44	£73	£15	£36	£25	£26

What were Paulo's takings for each day in Week 2?

2 Use your **answers** from question 1.
   In the third week Paulo's takings increased by:

Mon	Tue	Wed	Thu	Fri	Sat	Sun
£74	£24	£56	£17	£23	£34	£27

What were Paulo's takings for each day in Week 3?

3 (a) 134 + 77   (b) 668 + 64   (c) 895 + 46   (d) 286 + 57
   (e) 787 + 65   (f) 856 + 86   (g) 689 + 34   (h) 477 + 36

4 (a) 345 + ■ = 400   (b) 431 + ■ = 500   (c) 522 + ■ = 600
   (d) 727 + ■ = 800   (e) 964 + ■ = 1000   (f) 653 + ■ = 700

5 (a) 226 + ■ = 289   (b) 153 + ■ = 198   (c) 481 + ■ = 525
   (d) 765 + ■ = 850   (e) 874 + ■ = 927   (f) 342 + ■ = 435
   (g) 147 + ■ = 233   (h) 568 + ■ = 655   (i) 526 + ■ = 602

1 How many items are on each of these orders?

(a)
Ice-Cream Bar Order	
Cones	
chocolate	120
plain	140

(b)
Ice-Cream Bar Order	
Wafers	
nougat	230
plain	160

(c)
Ice-Cream Bar Order	
Tubs	
small	370
large	110

(d)
Ice-Cream Bar Order	
Spoons	
plastic	410
wooden	260

(e)
Ice-Cream Bar Order	
Napkins	
white	220
green	350

(f)
Ice-Cream Bar Order	
Dishes	
paper	190
plastic	310

2 (a) $360 + 350 = \blacksquare$ (b) $470 + 340 = \blacksquare$ (c) $160 + 180 = \blacksquare$
   (d) $240 + 170 = \blacksquare$ (e) $730 + 180 = \blacksquare$ (f) $420 + 290 = \blacksquare$
   (g) $230 + \blacksquare = 420$ (h) $570 + \blacksquare = 730$ (i) $\blacksquare + 360 = 620$

140 250 290 170 260 160 180 270

3 Find the total number of ice-creams sold.

  (a) chocolate   (b) raspberry
  (c) lemon   (d) orange

4 How many of these were sold?

  (a) raspberry and orange **cones**
  (b) lemon and chocolate **tubs**

5 What was the total number sold of

  (a) cones   (b) tubs?

6 (a) $230 + 270 + 220 = \blacksquare$
   (b) $160 + 250 + 340 = \blacksquare$

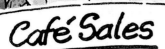

Café Sales

Cauliflower Combo 126
Bean Risotto 217
Vegetable Lasagne 163
Stuffed Peppers 154
Winter Salad 105
Vege-Stew 182

Carry-out Sales

Cauliflower Combo 220
Bean Risotto 180
Vegetable Lasagne 200
Stuffed Peppers 230
Winter Salad 160
Vege-Stew 210

1 What was the total number of each item sold?

(a) Cauliflower Combo   (b) Bean Risotto   (c) Vegetable Lasagne
(d) Stuffed Peppers   (e) Winter Salad   (f) Vege-Stew

2
(a) 316 + 280   (b) 150 + 136   (c) 170 + 211
(d) 465 + 120   (e) 530 + 128   (f) 359 + 340

3
(a) 123 + ■ = 293   (b) 110 + ■ = 344   (c) 138 + ■ = 588
(d) ■ + 240 = 571   (e) ■ + 326 = 456   (f) ■ + 420 = 562

4 How many cartons of these soups were sold?

(a) Parsnip and Carrot
(b) Tomato and Pumpkin
(c) Onion and Leek
(d) Carrot and Potato
(e) Leek and Bean
(f) Pumpkin and Onion
(g) Bean and Carrot
(h) Potato and Parsnip

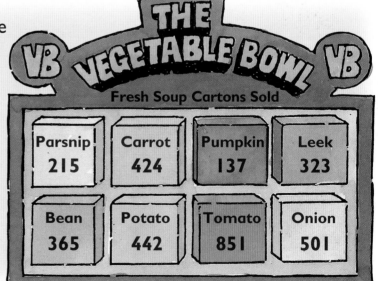

Fresh Soup Cartons Sold

Parsnip	Carrot	Pumpkin	Leek
215	424	137	323

Bean	Potato	Tomato	Onion
365	442	851	501

5
(a) 146 + ■ = 487   (b) 453 + ■ = 688   (c) 321 + ■ = 483
(d) ■ + 215 = 598   (e) ■ + 134 = 469   (f) ■ + 292 = 599

Week 1	Rent	Heating	Cleaning	Stock	Wages
Paulo's Pizza Parlour	£126	£245	£138	£347	£534
Ice-Cream Bar	£104	£239	£152	£356	£427
The Vegetable Bowl	£169	£213	£136	£438	£465

1 In Week 1 how much was spent

(a) by *Paulo's Pizza Parlour* on Heating and Cleaning
(b) by the *Ice-Cream Bar* on Wages and Stock
(c) by *The Vegetable Bowl* on Heating and Rent?

Week 2	Rent	Heating	Cleaning	Stock	Wages
Paulo's Pizza Parlour	£137	£228	£115	£329	£439
Ice-Cream Bar	£178	£254	£119	£418	£516
The Vegetable Bowl	£123	£247	£145	£427	£406

2 During Week 1 **and** Week 2 how much altogether did each snack bar pay for

(a) Rent   (b) Heating   (c) Cleaning   (d) Stock   (e) Wages?

3 In **Week 2** which snack bar spent

(a) £694 on Rent and Wages
(b) £557 on Heating and Stock
(c) £551 on Cleaning and Wages?

1 Add the bonus points to find each child's total score.

2 (a) 2568 + 20   (b) 70 + 5024   (c) 8018 + 90

   (d) 9402 + 80   (e) 5555 + 30   (f) 60 + 2033

   (g) 10 151 + 40   (h) 11 362 + 20   (i) 10 013 + 70

3 How many **bonus** points did each child score?

4 (a) 7246 + ■ = 7296   (b) 3054 + ■ = 3084   (c) 6161 + ■ = 6191

5 Josh scored 5315 points. Suzi scored 50 points more than Josh.
What was Suzi's score?

6 Mel scored 10 527 points.
When she added her bonus points her total was 10 587 points.
How many bonus points did she score?

Score **300 points** · Score **500 points** · Score **400 points** · Score **200 points** · Score **600 points**

1 Find each child's score.

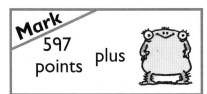 Mark 597 points plus

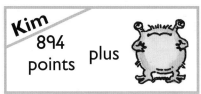 Kim 894 points plus

 Aisha 747 points plus

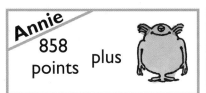 Annie 858 points plus

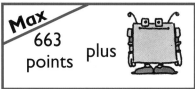 Max 663 points plus

 Darren 809 points plus

2 (a) $759 + 800$ (b) $336 + 900$ (c) $500 + 676$

(d) $634 + 400$ (e) $300 + 844$ (f) $927 + 200$

(g) $500 + 554$ (h) $417 + 700$ (i) $874 + 300$

3 How many points are on each child's card?

I had 878 points. I now have 1378 points. **Kelly**

I had 643 points. I now have 1243 points. **Jason**

4 (a) $676 + \blacksquare = 1276$ (b) $393 + \blacksquare = 1293$ (c) $\blacksquare + 972 = 1872$

(d) $700 + \blacksquare = 1204$ (e) $400 + \blacksquare = 1387$ (f) $\blacksquare + 300 = 1107$

5 Todd had a total of 9786 points.
Mai scored 400 points more than Todd.
What was Mai's total score?

CINEMA AUDIENCE FIGURES

	Multiplex	Film Centre	Picture Palace	Moviemall	Cityscreen
Weekdays (Mon – Thu)	3326	2253	1407	1716	3082
Weekend (Fri – Sun)	4485	3069	2614	2454	3925

1 How many people altogether went to see films at these cinemas on **Weekdays**?

(a) *Multiplex* and *Film Centre* (b) *Picture Palace* and *Cityscreen*
(c) *Film Centre* and *Moviemall* (d) *Cityscreen* and *Moviemall*

2 How many people altogether went to see films at these cinemas over the **Weekend**?

(a) *Film Centre* and *Cityscreen* (b) *Moviemall* and *Multiplex*
(c) *Picture Palace* and *Film Centre* (d) *Multiplex* and *Picture Palace*

3 What was the total number of people who saw films at each cinema on Weekdays **and** over the Weekend?

4 (a) 5648 + 2275 (b) 3639 + 4296 (c) 7493 + 2876
(d) 5959 + 1708 (e) 2656 + 6889 (f) 4513 + 3487

5 The table shows the number of seats in each of the 5 cinemas at the **Multiplex**. Each cinema has 3 film shows every day.
How many people altogether see films on a day when **all 5 cinemas are full for all 3 shows**?

Multiplex	Number of seats
Cinema 1	400
Cinema 2	350
Cinema 3	150
Cinema 4	100
Cinema 5	75

21

Ask your teacher how to play this game.

Target score

3286 plus 774 plus ☐ equals 6000.

Add 90 to 11983.

Find the total of 1886 and 3948.

Double ☐ is 152 000.

4616 + ☐ gives 7001.

Score

☐ 1 point

☐ 2 points

☐ 3 points

☐ 4 points

Find the sum of 2762 1715 and 2080.

Find the total of 123, 4, 56 and 7890.

Add 99, 87, 65, 43 and 21.

Each ☐ is the same **digit**. Find ☐.

☐☐4+6☐=286

3852 plus what gives 7452?

2380 add 3260 add 4120.

Find three consecutive numbers which total 600.

Add 277 to the sum of 414 and 236.

Each ☐ is the same **digit**. Find ☐.

☐0☐5 + ☐0 equals ☐145

Addition: problem solving and enquiry, calculators

TOPIC ASSESSMENT

Furniture and Carpet Sale

1 Find the **Sale price** of each item.

(a)

£730
Take £50 off

(b)

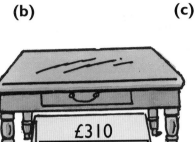

£310
Take £30 off

(c)

£520
Take £40 off

(d)

£845
Take £80 off

(e)

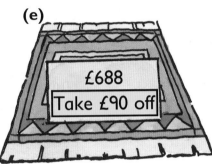

£688
Take £90 off

(f)

£457
Take £70 off

2 **(a)** £260 – £80   **(b)** £150 – £60   **(c)** £540 – £70

    (d) £913 – £30   **(e)** £369 – £90   **(f)** £616 – £50

    (g) £320 – £◼ = £260   **(h)** £◼ – £20 = £480   **(i)** £845 – £◼ = £785

3

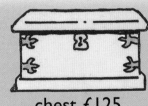

chest £125   stool £71   cabinet £240   lamp £58

Find the difference in price between the

    (a) cabinet and stool   **(b)** lamp and cabinet

    (c) stool and chest   **(d)** chest and lamp.

4 **(a)** £430 – £49   **(b)** £820 – £92   **(c)** £150 – £81

    (d) £906 – £88   **(e)** £625 – £41   **(f)** £714 – £39

    (g) £220 – £◼ = £189   **(h)** £400 – £◼ = £311   **(i)** £935 – £◼ = £884

CD CITY OUR TOP TEN

CD Title	CDs sold in January	February
a Much More Music	473	34
b Golden Oldies	154	27
c Dance Fever	260	32
d Disco Classics	67	296
e Club Mix	55	391
f Groove Masters	171	47
g Film Themes	182	56
h Rock Dinosaurs	86	194
i Jazz Jive	16	145
j Cool Rap	352	35

1 For each CD, find the difference between the number sold in January and in February.

2 (a) 875 – 27 (b) 692 – 24 (c) 567 – 18 (d) 283 – 65
(e) 364 – 45 (f) 385 – 77 (g) 190 – 43 (h) 474 – 58

3 How many places did each CD rise or fall in the UK Chart between January and February?

UK CHART PLACINGS

CD Title	January	February
a Love Songs	186	37
b Country Breeze	23	141
c Blue Soul	17	132
d Best of TV Soaps	100	84
e Heavy Hits	76	193

Museum of Local History

Sword - 538 years old

Helmet - 57 years old

Plate - 76 years old

Painting - 415 years old

Clock - 94 years old

Coin - 920 years old

1 How many years older is the

   (a) Sword than the Helmet   **(b)** Painting than the Clock
   (c) Coin than the Plate   **(d)** Sword than the Clock
   (e) Painting than the Plate   **(f)** Coin than the Helmet
   (g) Coin than the Clock   **(h)** Sword than the Plate
   (i) Painting than the Helmet?

2 **(a)** 146 – 65   **(b)** 329 – 43   **(c)** 617 – 35   **(d)** 268 – 87
    (e) 704 – 84   **(f)** 833 – 73   **(g)** 210 – 67   **(h)** 730 – 46
    (i) 111 – 27   **(j)** 351 – 83   **(k)** 634 – 67   **(l)** 805 – 36

3

Gold Watch – made 125 years ago.

Silver Watch – made 56 years **after** the Gold Watch.

How many years old is
(a) the Silver Watch
(b) the Brass Watch?

Brass Watch – made 37 years **after** the Gold Watch.

Hours of Sunshine					
	Port Ann	**Blue Coast**	**Long Point**	**Shell Bay**	**Cape Fire**
Spring	300	400	190	240	160
Summer	710	920	570	480	330

1 Find the difference in the hours of sunshine in **Spring** between
  (a) Port Ann and Long Point   **(b)** Blue Coast and Cape Fire
  (c) Shell Bay and Port Ann   **(d)** Shell Bay and Blue Coast
  (e) Long Point and Shell Bay   **(f)** Cape Fire and Shell Bay.

2 Find the difference in the hours of sunshine in the **Summer** between
  (a) Long Point and Shell Bay   **(b)** Blue Coast and Long Point
  (c) Long Point and Port Ann   **(d)** Port Ann and Cape Fire
  (e) Cape Fire and Long Point   **(f)** Shell Bay and Blue Coast.

3 In **Autumn**, Port Ann had 610 hours of sunshine.
Find the number of hours of sunshine at
  (a) Blue Coast ➤ 90 hours less than Port Ann
  (b) Long Point ➤ 280 hours less than Blue Coast
  (c) Shell Bay ➤ 150 hours less than Long Point
  (d) Cape Fire ➤ 670 hours less than Port Ann and Long Point **together.**

4 **(a)** $700 - \blacksquare = 390$ **(b)** $820 - \blacksquare = 550$
  (c) $530 - \blacksquare = 250$ **(d)** $940 - \blacksquare = 280$
  (e) $\blacksquare - 130 = 470$ **(f)** $\blacksquare - 290 = 160$

Subtraction: multiples of 10, with bridging   **HOME ACTIVITY 6**

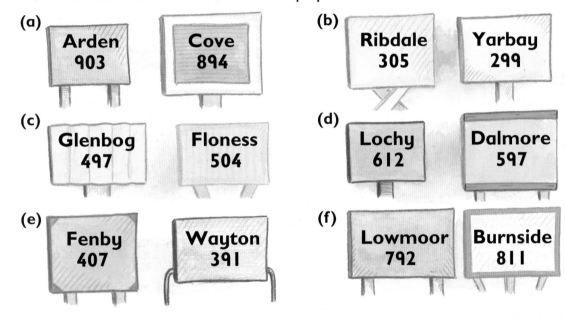

Welcome to Asham
Population 706

1 The population of **Benvale** is 688.
How many fewer people live in Benvale than in Asham?

2 Find the difference between these populations:

(a) Arden 903 Cove 894

(b) Ribdale 305 Yarbay 299

(c) Glenbog 497 Floness 504

(d) Lochy 612 Dalmore 597

(e) Fenby 407 Wayton 391

(f) Lowmoor 792 Burnside 811

3 (a) 802 – 693 (b) 406 – 298 (c) 905 – 398 (d) 604 – 295
(e) 703 – 486 (f) 507 – 189 (g) 314 – 196 (h) 913 – 597
(i) 505 – 289 (j) 816 – 397 (k) 615 – 398 (l) 708 – 489

4 Millburn's population is 17 greater than Deemouth's.
Newton's population is half of Millburn's.
How many people live in Newton?

Deemouth Population 793

1 Copy and complete Ming's work.

Ming
320 + 250 =
250 + 320 =
570 – 320 =
570 – 250 =

2 Use your answers in **question 1** to find

(a) 320 + 249   (b) 252 + 323
(c) 570 – 251   (d) 570 – 316

3 Write two addition **and** two subtraction stories using each set of numbers.

(a) 627 340 967

(b) 323 783 460

(c) 550 987 437

4 (a) Who has subtracted correctly? Check by **adding**.

Ravi
430 – 270 = 150

Gary
920 – 680 = 240

Katy
804 – 395 = 409

(b) For each **correct** subtraction, write
• the addition you used to check
• another addition you **could** use to check.

5 (a) Check each subtraction by adding.

751 – 274 = 477

846 – 359 = 477

934 – 457 = 477

(b) Write each **correct** subtraction and **two** additions you could use to check it.

1

Barnley School	Pipdale School	Forsham School	Sidburgh School
We have raised £846.	Our school has collected £2153.	Forsham has raised £1532.	We have collected £1980.

How much more money has been raised for the Appeal by

(a) Sidburgh than Barnley **(b)** Pipdale than Barnley

(c) Forsham than Barnley **(d)** Sidburgh than Forsham

(e) Pipdale than Forsham **(f)** Pipdale than Sidburgh?

2
(a) 3592 – 485	**(b)** 6114 – 931	**(c)** 7256 – 879
(d) 5463 – 2128	**(e)** 9706 – 1540	**(f)** 4377 – 2765
(g) 8730 – 4357	**(h)** 5627 – 2856	**(i)** 3064 – 1425
(j) 4371 – 2982	**(k)** 7153 – 5278	**(l)** 6050 – 3959

3 A total of £6511 has been raised so far for the *Wildlife Garden Appeal.*

How much more money is needed to reach the TARGET of £9000?

TARGET £9000

Wildlife Garden Appeal

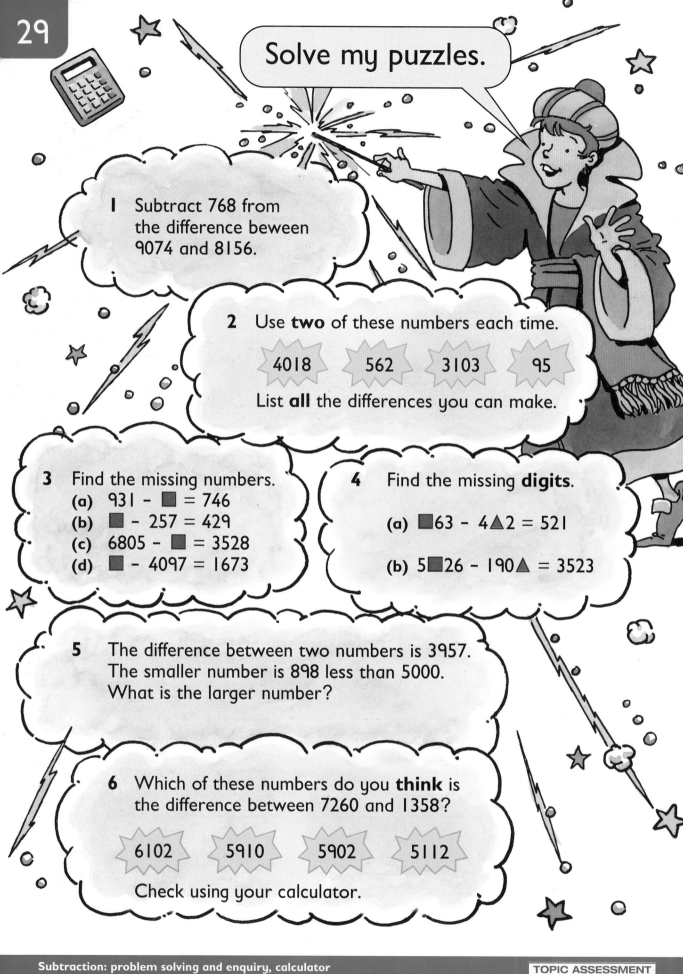

Solve my puzzles.

1 Subtract 768 from the difference beween 9074 and 8156.

2 Use **two** of these numbers each time.

4018   562   3103   95

List **all** the differences you can make.

3 Find the missing numbers.
(a) 931 – ■ = 746
(b) ■ – 257 = 429
(c) 6805 – ■ = 3528
(d) ■ – 4097 = 1673

4 Find the missing **digits**.

(a) ■63 – 4▲2 = 521

(b) 5■26 – 190▲ = 3523

5 The difference between two numbers is 3957. The smaller number is 898 less than 5000. What is the larger number?

6 Which of these numbers do you **think** is the difference between 7260 and 1358?

6102   5910   5902   5112

Check using your calculator.

Antique Sale

Painting £3600

Chair £300

Table £500

Clock £900

Sofa £1700

Rug £800

1 How much altogether would it cost to buy the

(a) Clock and Rug

(b) Chair and Clock

(c) Sofa and Chair

(d) Table and Painting

(e) Clock and Sofa

(f) Painting and Rug

(g) Clock and Painting

(h) Sofa and Rug

(i) Chair, Table and Rug?

2 (a) $800 + 300$ (b) $400 + 600$ (c) $700 + 700$

(d) $7500 + 700$ (e) $500 + 2900$ (f) $4800 + 800$

(g) $400 + 900 + 200$ (h) $300 + 1200 + 400$

3 (a) $900 + \blacksquare = 1800$ (b) $\blacksquare + 800 = 1300$

(c) $5600 + \blacksquare = 6200$ (d) $\blacksquare + 7700 = 8100$

1 Find each ticket number.

Anna
My number is the sum of 2700 and 900.

Rory
To make my number you double 900 and then add 500.

Su
My number is double Anna's number.

Ben
My number is the total of 30 and 2158.

David
My number is 300 more than Ben's.

Ravi
My number is double the sum of 500, 400 and 800.

Jane
My number is 43 more than Rory's.

Marie
When you add 600 to my number, you get 3000.

2 Whose ticket numbers have a difference of **(a)** 100 **(b)** 200?

3 The **winning** ticket number
- has the same tens and units digit
- is between two thousand and three thousand
- has a hundreds digit which is double its thousands digit
- has no zero.

Who has the winning ticket?

1 How many fruits are left?

(a)

1400

Eat 6.

(b)

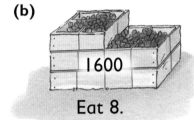

1600

Eat 8.

(c)

1300

Eat 5.

(d)

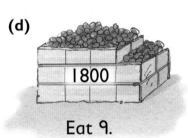

1800

Eat 9.

(e)

1500

Eat 4.

(f)

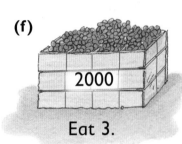

2000

Eat 3.

2 **(a)** 5 less than 1482   **(b)** Subtract 8 from 1364.

(c) 2575 minus 7   **(d)** Take 3 from 5211.

(e) 3147 take away 9   **(f)** 6 less than 7293

(g) Subtract 4 from 1402.   **(f)** Take 8 from 4706.

(i) 1003 subtract 5   **(j)** 2006 minus 7

3 **(a)** 2164 − ■ = 2159 **(b)** 2282 − ■ = 2279

(c) ■ − 6 = 4245   **(d)** ■ − 8 = 1548

(e) 3358 − ■ = 3349 **(f)** 4673 − ■ = 4669

(g) ■ − 7 = 6315   **(h)** ■ − 9 = 1234

Franka's Fruit Factory

Raspberry Jam | Plum Jam | Apple Juice | Orange Juice | Strawberries | Peaches

4000 | 3992 | 2000 | 1996 | 3000 | 2994

1 Find the difference between the number of

(a) jars of raspberry jam and plum jam

(b) cartons of apple juice and orange juice

(c) tins of strawberries and peaches.

2 (a) 2364 − 2358   (b) 6541 − 6535   (c) 3793 − 3784

    (d) 8132 − 8127   (e) 4305 − 4299   (f) 7803 − 7796

3 Find the difference between the number of cartons.

(a)

1998   2006

(b)

2997   3003

(c)

2003   1994

(d)

3002   2998

4 Find the difference between

(a) 5243 and 5229   (b) 9458 and 9474   (c) 2602 and 2587

(d) 6885 and 6901   (e) 4007 and 3994   (f) 4989 and 5005.

5 (a) 4702 − ■ = 4685   (b) 1007 − ■ = 995   (c) 2006 − ■ = 1998

    (d) ■ − 15 = 2586   (e) ■ − 14 = 1997   (f) ■ − 19 = 3987

Ask your teacher how to play this game for two players.

1500	1300	1100	1600	1200	1400
700	900	500	600	400	800
1400	1300	1520	1653	1721	1200
7	5	8	9	6	4
1995	1990	1999	1987	1989	1997
2006	2002	2010	2008	2004	2011

1 Janey found 3 boxes of old coins.

   (a) How many coins did she find altogether?

   (b) She gave Sam half of the silver coins and one quarter of the gold coins. How many coins does she have left?

   (c) How many more coins would Janey need to make a total of 4000 coins?

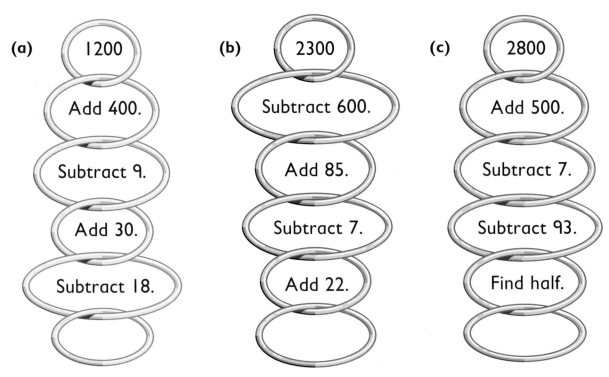

2 Use + **or** − each time.

Copy and complete.

(a)
  1900 ● 600 = 2500
  2009 ● 1992 = 17
  3000 ● 8 = 2992

(b)
  2175 ● 18 = 2193
  3265 ● 8 = 3257
  1359 ● 600 = 759

3 Find the number at the bottom of each chain.

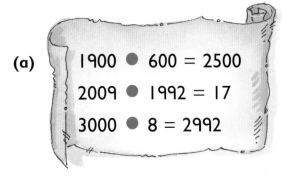

(a) 1200
Add 400.
Subtract 9.
Add 30.
Subtract 18.

(b) 2300
Subtract 600.
Add 85.
Subtract 7.
Add 22.

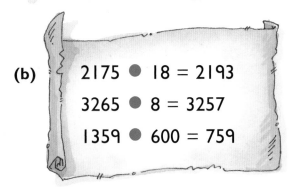

(c) 2800
Add 500.
Subtract 7.
Subtract 93.
Find half.

1 Tickets for *International Sportslinks* events are sold in **books of 100**.
How many tickets have been sold for each of these events?

(a) long jump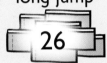

(b) triple jump

(c) high jump

(d) hurdles

(e) pole vault

(f) javelin

(g) marathon

(h) 400 metres

(i) 100 metres

2 What do you notice about your answers in question 1?

3 (a) $100 \times 238 = \blacksquare$ (b) $100 \times 96 = \blacksquare$ (c) $341 \times 100 = \blacksquare$

   (d) $100 \times 16 = \blacksquare$ (e) $100 \times 107 = \blacksquare$ (f) $54 \times 100 = \blacksquare$

4 (a) $100 \times \blacksquare = 3500$ (b) $100 \times \blacksquare = 12\,300$ (c) $100 \times \blacksquare = 1900$

   (d) $\blacksquare \times 100 = 4100$ (e) $\blacksquare \times 100 = 9200$ (f) $\blacksquare \times 100 = 10\,400$

5

Pool events
10 sheets of tickets
10 tickets on each sheet

How many sheets and how many tickets were sold for these events?

(a) swimming – 63 books
(b) diving – 159 books

I Programmes for the events are packed in **boxes of 200**.
How many programmes are there for each of these events?

(a) rowing
80 boxes

(b) canoeing
30 boxes

(c) sailing
50 boxes

(d) water ski-ing
20 boxes

(e) surfing
90 boxes

(f) wind-surfing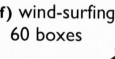
60 boxes

2 Explain how you found the answers in question **I**.

3 **(a)** Multiply 10 by 200. **(b)** 40 multiplied by 200
 (c) 70 times 200 **(d)** 200 times double 25

4 **(a)** 300 × 10 **(b)** 800 × 90 **(c)** 60 × 400
 (d) 900 × 50 **(e)** 400 × 20 **(f)** 40 × 300
 (g) 500 × 80 **(h)** 600 × 40 **(i)** 70 × 700
 (j) 700 × 80 **(k)** 600 × 30 **(l)** 30 × 500

5 **(a)** Multiply 500 by 60, then add 400.
 (b) Find 70 muliplied by 400, then add 200.
 (c) Find 30 times 900, then subtract 700.
 (d) Multiply 50 by 600 and 20 by 800.
  Add the two products.
 (e) Find 80 multiplied by 600 and 40 multiplied by 900.
  What is the difference between the two products?

1 Find the cost **in Euros** of

(a) 7    (b) 5    (c) 10    (d) 9

(e) 6    (f) 4    (g) 8    (h) 6

(i) 9  and 7    (j) 5 and 9

(k) 8  and 4    (l) 7 and 9

2
(a) 3 × 8	(b) 4 × 4	(c) 7 × 5	(d) 9 × 9
(e) 8 × 5	(f) 6 × 8	(g) 7 × 9	(h) 8 × 2
(i) 10 × 10	(j) 0 × 6	(k) 9 × 4	(l) 7 × 7
(m) 8 × 9	(n) 7 × 8	(o) 10 × 7	(p) 9 × 8

3
(a) 6 × ■ = 42	(b) 9 × ■ = 18	(c) ■ × 8 = 80	(d) ■ × 3 = 15
(e) 4 × ■ = 0	(f) 5 × ■ = 30	(g) ■ × 6 = 24	(h) ■ × 4 = 20

 4 Maxine spent a total of €120.
She bought **two** kinds of souvenirs.

Which souvenirs and how many
of each could she have bought?
Explain.

 **$8**  **$5**  **$9**  **$7**  **$6**

1 How much would it cost to buy

(a) 4   (b) 10   (c) 8

(d) 7   (e) 9   (f) 6

(g) 10   (h) 3   (i) 4

(j) 3   (k) 7   (l) 5

2 The Rocky Mountain Company prints 8 posters in one minute.

How many posters can they print in

(a) 5 minutes (b) 9 minutes
(c) 3 minutes (d) 8 minutes
(e) 10 minutes (f) 6 minutes?

3 Find the product of each pair of numbers.

(a)  5 10 (b)  4 7 (c) 8 4

(d) 3 0 (e)  7 9 (f) 7 5

4 List pairs of numbers with a product of

(a) 12 (b) 20 (c) 36 (d) 40

5 List **three** numbers with a product of 30.

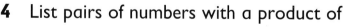

For every **one** computer game I have, Amy has **two.**

1 (a) When Wesley has 9 games, how many does Amy have?
(b) When Amy has 16 games, how many does Wesley have?

2 How many games do they have **altogether** when

(a) Wesley has 7 (b) Amy has 10?

For every **three** CDs I have, Terry has **one.**

3 Write True (T) or False (F).

(a) Jane has three times as many CDs as Terry.
(b) Terry has one third of the **total** number of CDs.
(c) When Terry has 5 CDs, Jane has 15.
(d) When Jane has 36 CDs, Terry has 9.

4 The Music Club has 3 boys for every 2 girls.
There are 27 boys at the Club.
How many girls are there?

5 The Dance Club has 5 times as many girls as boys.
There are 20 boys at the Club.
How many girls are there?

6 The Games Club has 6 boys for every 4 girls.
There are 12 girls at the Club.
How many **children** are there?

I drive 75 miles every **day**.

I run 43 miles a week.

I walk 36 miles a week.

I cycle 28 miles each week.

Rob   **Jan**   **Martha**   **Alan**

1 How many miles does

(a) Jan run in 6 weeks

(b) Alan cycle in 8 weeks

(c) Martha walk in 9 weeks

(d) Rob drive in 1 **week**?

2 Who travels more miles, Alan in 9 weeks or Martha in 7 weeks?

3 (a) 6 × 81   (b) 8 × 17   (c) 7 × 62   (d) 9 × 54

(e) 7 × 39   (f) 6 × 55   (g) 9 × 26   (h) 8 × 48

4

For the next eight weeks I will run an extra nine miles each week.

How many miles will Jan run in these eight weeks?

Jan

£1 can be exchanged for:

2 Swiss Francs

3 Brazilian Real

4 New Zealand Dollars

9 South African Rand
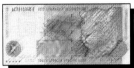

1 How much money should each person receive?

(a)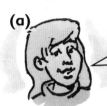
Forty three pounds in Dollars.

(b)
Twenty-four pounds in Real.

(c)
Sixty-two pounds in Francs.

(d)
Thirty-one pounds in Rand.

2 Exchange each of these amounts for

- Brazilian Real
- South African Rand.

(a) £42   (b) £53   (c) £83   (d) £65

3 (a) 5×74 (b) 6×58 (c) 37×8 (d) 7×92
   (e) 8×29 (f) 67×7 (g) 6×86 (h) 5×99

4 **50p** can be exchanged for:

7 Mexican Pesos

6 Danish Kroner

How much money should Claire receive when she exchanges

(a) £33 for Danish Kroner   (b) £47 for Mexican Pesos?

International Trade Fair

1 What is the cost of 20 of each?

 (a) Maple Syrup   **(b)** Coffee   **(c)** Wool
 (d) Cotton   **(e)** Tea   **(f)** Rice

2 **(a)** $20 \times 12 = \blacksquare$ **(b)** $20 \times 19 = \blacksquare$ **(c)** $11 \times 20 = \blacksquare$
 (d) $20 \times \blacksquare = 260$ **(e)** $\blacksquare \times 20 = 320$ **(f)** $20 \times \blacksquare = 400$

3 How much did each person spend?

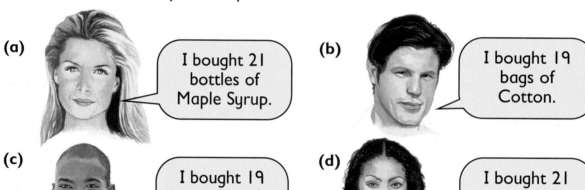

 (a) I bought 21 bottles of Maple Syrup.

 (b) I bought 19 bags of Cotton.

 (c) I bought 19 cartons of Wool.

 (d) I bought 21 sacks of Rice.

 (e) I bought 21 bags of Coffee.

 (f) I bought 19 crates of Tea.

4 **(a)** 19×22 **(b)** 21×32 **(c)** 23×19 **(d)** 21×34
 (e) 19×28 **(f)** 26×21 **(g)** 19×25 **(h)** 21×39

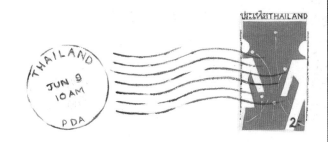

1 **(a)** 5×18 **(b)** 5×24 **(c)** 32×5 **(d)** 15×14
(e) 15×16 **(f)** 18×15 **(g)** 25×12 **(h)** 25×16
(i) 18×25 **(j)** 46×5 **(k)** 45×18 **(l)** 14×35

2 Which is greater and by how much?

(a) 15×20 or 25×14
(b) 35×16 or 45×12
(c) 5×82 or 25×16

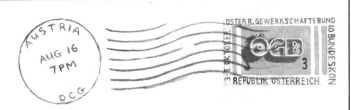

3 **(a)** 14×13 **(b)** 12×22 **(c)** 16×21 **(d)** 14×11
(e) 16×17 **(f)** 18×13 **(g)** 14×24 **(h)** 18×17
(i) 12×38 **(j)** 16×29 **(k)** 18×11 **(l)** 12×19

4 Find the missing numbers.

(a) Multiply ■ by 12 and the product is 168.
(b) Multiply ■ by 16 and the product is 176.

Oil 597 ℓ   **Diesel** 425 ℓ   **Petrol** 653 ℓ   **Paraffin** 308 ℓ

1 How many litres of fuel are in

  (a) 2 drums of Paraffin **(b)** 4 drums of Diesel **(c)** 3 drums of Oil
  (d) 6 drums of Petrol **(e)** 7 drums of Oil **(f)** 9 drums of Petrol?

2 Which holds more

  (a) 3 drums of Paraffin   or 2 drums of Diesel
  (b) 5 drums of Oil   or 8 drums of Paraffin
  (c) 4 drums of Petrol   or 6 drums of Oil
  (d) 9 drums of Diesel   or 7 drums of Petrol?

windscreen £183   headlight £256   brakes £435   fuel tank £898   exhaust £324   tyre £317

3 How much does Mr Brown pay for

  (a) 8 headlights   **(b)** 3 fuel tanks   **(c)** 5 sets of brakes?

4 Which of these cost **between** £1500 and £1750?

  (a) 5 exhausts **(b)** 9 windscreens **(c)** 2 fuel tanks
  (d) 6 tyres **(e)** 3 headlights **(f)** 4 sets of brakes

5 Mr Brown has £3500 to spend.
Is it possible for him to buy 4 windscreens, 4 headlights and 4 sets of brakes? Explain.

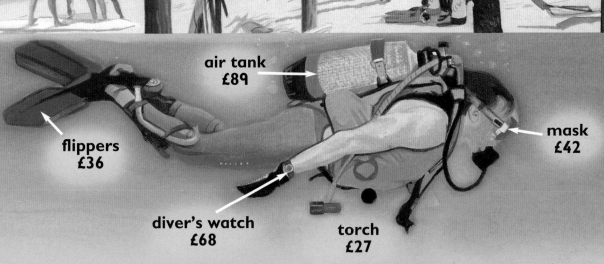

air tank
£89

flippers
£36

mask
£42

diver's watch
£68

torch
£27

1 What does the Watersports Centre pay for

(a) 23 masks   (b) 16 air tanks   (c) 52 pairs of flippers

(d) 44 torches   (e) 37 watches?

2 How much money did the Watersports Centre earn from these courses?

(a) parascending ➔ 13 people
(b) wind-surfing ➔ 32 people
(c) scuba-diving ➔ 24 people
(d) dinghy-sailing ➔ 28 people
(e) water-skiing ➔ 46 people

Coral Beach Watersports Centre Training Courses

scuba-diving	£74
parascending	£95
wind-surfing	£43
dinghy-sailing	£51
water-skiing	£39

3

(a) 66×55 (b) 58×71 (c) 94×26 (d) 49×53

(e) 87×41 (f) 75×67 (g) 59×92 (h) 83×64

Monster Party

Ricky: I saved 75p every week for one year.

Gita: I saved 60p every week for a year and a half.

1   How much money did each child save for the party?

2   Ricky will be 10 years old on his birthday.
    Has he lived for more than 90 000 hours? Explain.

3   There are 125 children at the Monster Party.
    Every child receives one of each of these items.

   (a) 38p   (b)   27p   (c) 18p   (d)  84p

   Find the total cost for each item.

4 | Birthday Cake | |
    | --- | --- |
    | Icing | 375 g |
    | Flour | 650 g |
    | Butter | 225 g |
    | Sultanas | 125 g |
    | Cherries | 95 g |
    | Sugar | 160 g |

   45 Birthday cakes are baked for the party.
   Find the total weight of each ingredient used.

5   Solve these Puzzle Cards from the Birthday Bags.

   (a) Use these digits to make a
       two-digit number and a
       three-digit number which give
       • the largest possible product
       • the smallest possible product.

   1 2 3 4 5

   (b) Find the missing number.

   $15 \times 60 + \blacksquare = 960$

   (c) Which number, multiplied by **itself**, gives a product of 625?

1 Sandie makes 24 cheese sandwiches.
Each tray holds 8 sandwiches.
How many trays can she fill?

2 How many trays can Sandie fill with these sandwiches?

(a)  35 sandwiches,
7 in each tray.

(b)  72 sandwiches,
9 in each tray.

(c)  40 sandwiches,
5 in each tray.

(d)  70 sandwiches,
10 in each tray.

(e)  20 sandwiches,
4 in each tray.

(f)  18 sandwiches,
6 in each tray.

3 **(a)** Divide 54 by 9.
(c) Zero divided by 3
(e) Divide 72 by 8.
(g) Half of 14

(b) Share 14 equally among 7.
(d) How many tens make 100?
(f) 20 divided equally among 5
(h) How many groups of six are in 30?

4 **(a)** $7 \div 7 = \blacksquare$ **(b)** $80 \div 10 = \blacksquare$ **(c)** $56 \div 8 = \blacksquare$ **(d)** $28 \div 4 = \blacksquare$
(e) $\blacksquare \div 9 = 9$ **(f)** $\blacksquare \div 5 = 0$ **(g)** $\blacksquare \div 10 = 4$ **(h)** $\blacksquare \div 8 = 4$
(i) $42 \div \blacksquare = 6$ **(j)** $45 \div \blacksquare = 5$ **(k)** $12 \div \blacksquare = 2$ **(l)** $80 \div \blacksquare = 10$

5 How many **free** sandwiches will
Sandie's Special Offer give with

(a) 24 sandwiches **(b)** 54 sandwiches
(c) 36 sandwiches **(d)** 60 sandwiches?

Sandie's Sandwiches
Special Offer
Buy 6 Get 1 extra
Free!

1 Divide the sandwiches equally among the trays.

(a)
60
10 trays

(b)
42
6 trays

(c)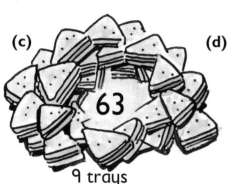
63
9 trays

(d)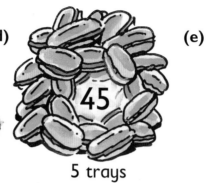
45
5 trays

(e)
27
3 trays

2 (a) $\dfrac{18}{9} = \blacksquare$ (b) $\dfrac{50}{10} = \blacksquare$ (c) $\dfrac{0}{6} = \blacksquare$ (d) $\dfrac{28}{7} = \blacksquare$

    (e) $\dfrac{\blacksquare}{2} = 9$ (f) $\dfrac{\blacksquare}{9} = 4$ (g) $\dfrac{\blacksquare}{4} = 1$ (h) $\dfrac{\blacksquare}{10} = 2$

    (i) $\dfrac{27}{\blacksquare} = 3$ (j) $\dfrac{90}{\blacksquare} = 10$ (k) $\dfrac{48}{\blacksquare} = 8$ (l) $\dfrac{90}{\blacksquare} = 10$

3 How many pickles can you buy when you spend
    (a) 21p   (b) 63p   (c) 49p   (d) 70p?

4 How many sauces can you buy when you spend
    (a) 48p   (b) 16p   (c) 40p   (d) 64p?

5 Tom bought **one third** as many pickles as Alexa.
    Together their pickles cost 56p.
    How many pickles did they each buy?

1 Simon Smith orders 300 address labels in **strips of 10.**

How many strips does he order?

2 How many strips of 10 can be made with

   (a) 500 labels   **(b)** 2000 labels
   (c) 4600 labels   **(d)** 7300 labels?

S. Smith
Weaver's
Cottage
Greenvale XY32

3 **(a)** ▢ ÷ 10 = 80   **(b)** ▢ ÷ 10 = 600   **(c)** ▢ ÷ 10 = 250   **(d)** ▢ ÷ 10 = 940

Amy Arnott
Flat 142
North Block
Oldburgh

4 Amy Arnott orders 600 address labels in **sheets of 100.**

How many sheets does she order?

5 How many sheets of 100 can be made with

   (a) 400 labels   **(b)** 9000 labels
   (c) 1800 labels   **(d)** 8700 labels?

6 **(a)** ▢ ÷ 100 = 9   **(b)** ▢ ÷ 100 = 40   **(c)** ▢ ÷ 100 = 59   **(d)** ▢ ÷ 100 = 31

7 Martin Moore orders 7000 address labels in **packets of 1000.**

How many packets does he order?

8 How many packets of 1000 can be made with

   (a) 5000 labels   **(b)** 8000 labels
   (c) 3000 labels   **(d)** 9000 labels?

M. Moore
Pathend House
Ringway AB65

9 **(a)** 200 ÷ 10 = ▢   **(b)** 4000 ÷ 1000 = ▢   **(c)** 700 ÷ 100 = ▢
   (d) 1700 ÷ 10 = ▢   **(e)** 3000 ÷ 100 = ▢   **(f)** 1000 ÷ 1000 = ▢
   (g) 6200 ÷ 100 = ▢   **(h)** 8800 ÷ 10 = ▢   **(i)** 9800 ÷ ▢ = 98
   (j) 6000 ÷ ▢ = 6   **(k)** 5200 ÷ ▢ = 520   **(l)** 4300 ÷ ▢ = 43

1 **(a)** List all the balloon numbers which divide exactly by 4.

   (b) Divide the **last two digits** of each number on your list by 4. What do you notice?

   (c) Describe a quick way to find if a number divides exactly by 4.

   (d) Use your quick way to find which of these numbers divide exactly by 4.

2

A leap year divides exactly by four.

Which of these are leap years?

(a) 1948

(b) 2008

(c) 1833

Investigations File

3 Write a fact about the **last digit** of a number that divides exactly by

   (a) 10   **(b)** 5   **(c)** 2

4 Write a fact about the **last two digits** of a number that divides exactly by 100.

1 For each calculation, use the numbers to write another three multiplication or division stories.

(a) $56 \div 7 = 8$ (b) $6 \times 9 = 54$ (c) $150 \div 6 = 25$

(d) $10 \times 60 = 600$ (e) $94 \div 2 = 47$ (f) $4 \times 26 = 104$

(g) $221 \div 13 = 17$ (h) $12 \times 23 = 276$ (i) $770 \div 35 = 22$

2

For each set of numbers, write two multiplications **and** two divisions.

(a) 42   7   6   (b) 20   4   80   (c) 5   55   11

(d) 300   10   30   (e) 25   450   18   (f) 19   15   285

3 Use the numbers 27, 43 and **one other number** to write four multiplications or divisions.

1 Check Myra's answers by **multiplying**.
Correct any that are wrong.

Name: Myra

(a) 168 ÷ 7 = 24   (b) 288 ÷ 9 = 31

(c) 324 ÷ 12 = 27   (d) 352 ÷ 8 = 44

(e) 208 ÷ 13 = 15   (f) 266 ÷ 14 = 19

(g) 735 ÷ 21 = 33   (h) 782 ÷ 17 = 45

(i) 676 ÷ 26 = 26   (j) 1520 ÷ 40 = 38

2 Copy and complete each division and write a **multiplication** that can
be used to check it.

(a) 222 ÷ 6 = ■   (b) 162 ÷ ■ = 18
(c) ■ ÷ 15 = 33   (d) 517 ÷ 11 = ■
(e) 525 ÷ ■ = 25   (f) ■ ÷ 28 = 30
(g) 924 ÷ ■ = 22   (h) 1568 ÷ 32 = ■
(i) ■ ÷ 48 = 48   (j) 2160 ÷ ■ = 54

3 Which two box numbers
divide to give

(a) 20   (b) 30
(c) a number on **another** box
(d) a number that is on
one of the two boxes?

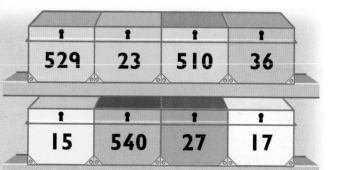

529   23   510   36

15   540   27   17

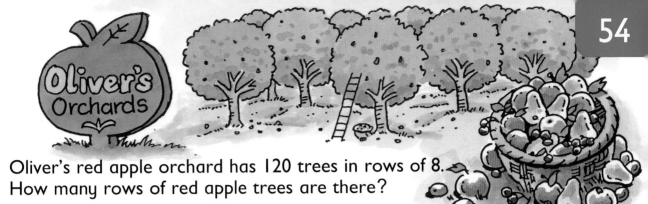

1 Oliver's red apple orchard has 120 trees in rows of 8.
How many rows of red apple trees are there?

2 How many rows of trees are in these orchards?

	Green apple	Pear	Red cherry	Black cherry	Plum
Number of trees	117	133	108	153	144
Number in each row	9	7	6	9	8

3 **(a)** 105 ÷ 7   **(b)** 108 ÷ 9   **(c)** 152 ÷ 8   **(d)** 144 ÷ 9

4 Oliver grows 184 strawberry plants in 8 equal rows.
How many plants are in each row?

5 These bushes are planted in equal rows.
How many bushes are in each row?

(a) 175 red currant — 7 rows

(b) 198 blackberry — 9 rows

(c) 148 raspberry — 4 rows

(d) 117 blackcurrant - in 3 rows   **(e)** 112 bramble - in 2 rows
(f) 265 gooseberry - in 5 rows   **(g)** 450 loganberry - in 6 rows
(h) 117 bilberry - in 8 rows   **(i)** 616 blueberry - in 7 rows

6 **(a)** 452 ÷ 4   **(b)** 354 ÷ 3   **(c)** 912 ÷ 8   **(d)** 702 ÷ 6
   (e) 648 ÷ 3   **(f)** 860 ÷ 4   **(g)** 663 ÷ 3   **(h)** 456 ÷ 2
   (i) 878 ÷ 2   **(j)** 972 ÷ 3   **(k)** 765 ÷ 5   **(l)** 944 ÷ 4

1   Oliver divides baskets of fruit equally amoung his trailers.
    How many baskets are on each trailer and how many are left over?

	Red apples	Green apples	Pears	Plums	Black cherries	Red cherries
Number of baskets	114	169	124	131	143	118
Number of trailers	8	9	7	8	9	6

2   Trays of fruit are packed in boxes and sent to the supermarkets.

    How many boxes can be **filled** with trays?

    How many trays are left over?

	Red apples	Green apples	Pears	Plums	Black cherries	Red cherries
Number of trays	118	174	157	195	220	175
Trays in each box	5	7	3	4	6	2

3   (a) 564 ÷ 5   (b) 818 ÷ 7   (c) 929 ÷ 7   (d) 770 ÷ 6
    (e) 907 ÷ 4   (f) 709 ÷ 3   (g) 943 ÷ 2   (h) 857 ÷ 3

4   Oliver divides 151 baskets of fruit amoung 8 trailers.
    One trailer has 7 baskets more than each of the others.

    How many baskets of fruit are on each trailer?

1 How much money does each child have?

2 Write in order, starting with the **largest** amount.

(a) £7·03, £6·85, £7·00, £6·98   (b) £10·30, £11·26, £9·72, £10·03

(c) £14·08, £15·18, £14·66, £14·80   (d) £19·70, £20·05, £19·07, £20·00

3 List the notes and coins for the amounts spent.

Gita £7·91   MEL £13·37   Zoë £19·66   Sam £11·88

4 Choose from these notes and coins. List five different ways of making £20.

1 How much money does each child have, **to the nearest pound**?

2 Round each amount **to the nearest pound**.

(a) £6·98 (b) £3·72 (c) £12·24 (d) £16·80

(e) £19·09 (f) £13·45 (g) £14·55 (h) £15·61

3

 £11·30  £4·79  £7·15  £5·95

Round the prices to the nearest pound and **estimate** the total cost of

(a) Mousetrap and Battleships (b) Battleships and 4 in-a-row

(c) Mousetrap, 4 in-a-row and Battleships

(d) Mousetrap, Battleships and Beat-the-Clock.

4 **Explain your answer each time**.

Use the prices rounded to the nearest pound. **Estimate** if you can buy

(a) Beat-the-Clock and 4 in-a-row with a £10 note

(b) Battleships, 4 in-a-row and Beat-the-Clock with a £20 note.

1 Find the total cost of.

(a) , and

(b) , and

(c) , and

(d) , and

(e) , , and

(f) 3

(g) 4

(h) 3

(i) 4

2 Zoë buys 3 different items.
She spends £2·90.
What could she buy?

3 Sami buys 4 items altogether.
He spends between £9 and £10.
What could he buy?

4 (a) £1·70 + ▢ = £2·40
(b) £1·10 + ▢ = £2·30
(c) £2·60 + ▢ = £3·50
(d) £3·50 + ▢ = £5·00

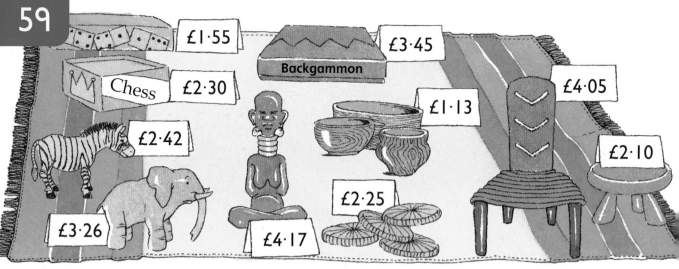

£1·55
£3·45
Backgammon
Chess £2·30
£4·05
£1·13
£2·42
£2·10
£2·25
£3·26
£4·17

1 Find the total cost of

(a) and

(b) and

(c) and

(d)  and

(e)  and

(f) and

(g) and and

(h)  and and

2 Suzi spent £3·65 altogether.
She bought and one other item.

What was the other item she bought?

3 Find the total cost of

(a) a zebra and a bowl

(b) a statue and an elephant

(c) a bowl and an elephant

(d) a zebra and a statue

(e) an elephant and a zebra

(f) a statue and a bowl.

4 Anja bought 2 bowls, a statue and an elephant.
How much did she spend altogether?

1 List the coins in each person's change.

(a) £20 £12·50

(b) £20 £16·40

(c) £20 £14·65

(d) £20 £11·15

(e) £20 £17·66

(f) £20 £13·73

2 How much does each person have left?

(a) I had £20.
I spent £13·50.

(b) I had £20.
I spent £9·35.

(c) I had £20.
I spent £11·59.

(d) I had £20.
I spent £16·84.

3 David bought a T-shirt. He paid with a £20 note.

His change was

How much did he spend?

4 Alana bought a book. She paid with a £20 note.
Her change was

How much did she spend?

African Wildlife Exhibition

Entrance

Adults   £4·50
Children £2·60

Jack
Fran   Ben Mia Jay

1 How much did it cost for the group to visit the exhibition?

2 Jack bought 3 animal pictures.

£4·25 each

   (a) How much did they cost altogether?

   (b) What was Jack's change from £20?

3 Jay had saved eight 50p coins and six 20p coins for the visit. How much had he saved altogether?

4 Mia spent one half of her savings on a book. The book cost £4·75. How much had she saved?

African Animals

5 Ben spent one quarter of his savings on a video. He had saved £16·40. How much did the video cost?

Africa

6 Fran spent £2·54 on drinks, £3·12 on food and £4·38 on gifts. Will she be able to pay using a £10 note? Explain your answer.

African Wildlife Exhibition

1 How many shapes in each set are coloured?

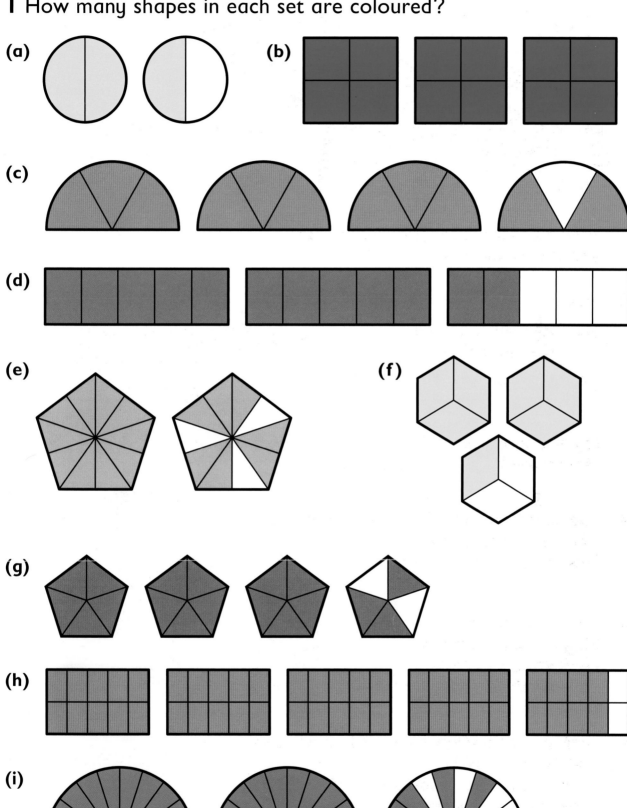

(a) (b) (c) (d) (e) (f) (g) (h) (i)

1 What fraction of each shape is coloured?

(a) 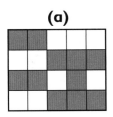 (b) 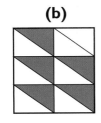 (c) 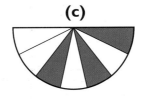 (d)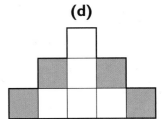

(e) 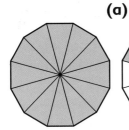 (f) 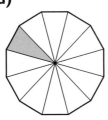 (g) 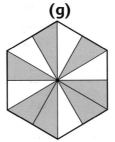 (h)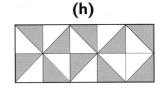

2 How many shapes in each set are coloured?

(a) (b)

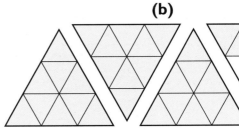

(c)

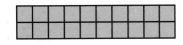 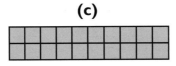 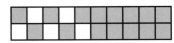

3 Write as an improper fraction.

(a) $2\frac{4}{20}$ (b) $3\frac{2}{7}$ (c) $4\frac{7}{9}$ (d) $2\frac{10}{12}$ (e) $1\frac{19}{20}$ (f) $5\frac{5}{9}$

4 Write as a mixed number.

(a) $\frac{64}{9}$ (b) $\frac{61}{20}$ (c) $\frac{83}{9}$ (d) $\frac{19}{7}$ (e) $\frac{100}{20}$ (f) $\frac{50}{12}$

I Copy and complete each equal fractions story.

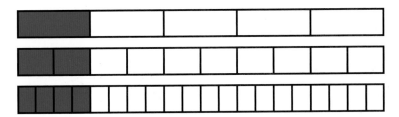

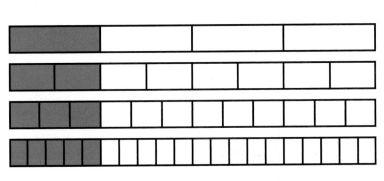

(a) $\dfrac{\blacksquare}{5} = \dfrac{\blacksquare}{10} = \dfrac{\blacksquare}{\blacksquare}$

(b) $\dfrac{1}{\blacksquare} = \dfrac{\blacksquare}{8} = \dfrac{3}{\blacksquare} = \dfrac{\blacksquare}{\blacksquare}$

(c) $\dfrac{\blacksquare}{9} = \dfrac{\blacksquare}{\blacksquare} = \dfrac{\blacksquare}{9} = \dfrac{\blacksquare}{\blacksquare}$

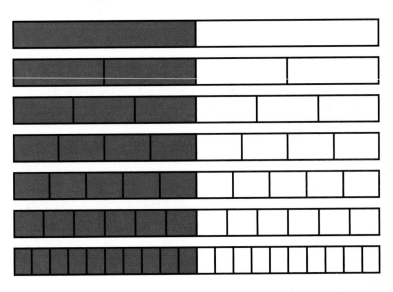

(d) $\dfrac{1}{2} = \dfrac{\blacksquare}{\blacksquare} = \dfrac{\blacksquare}{\blacksquare} = \dfrac{\blacksquare}{\blacksquare} = \dfrac{\blacksquare}{\blacksquare} = \dfrac{\blacksquare}{\blacksquare} = \dfrac{\blacksquare}{\blacksquare}$

Fractions: equivalence

One quarter is half of one half.

1 Copy and complete.

(a) One eighth is ___ of one quarter.

(b) One tenth is half of one ___.

(c) One ___ is half of one third.

(d) One twelfth is half of one ___ .

(e) One ___ is half of one tenth.

2

One half is more than one quarter.

One sixth is less than one third.

Write < or > between each pair of fractions.

(a) $\frac{1}{5}$ and $\frac{1}{10}$ (b) $\frac{1}{20}$ and $\frac{1}{12}$ (c) $\frac{1}{8}$ and $\frac{1}{9}$ (d) $\frac{1}{9}$ and $\frac{1}{12}$

(e) $\frac{1}{4}$ and $\frac{1}{5}$ (f) $\frac{1}{8}$ and $\frac{1}{7}$ (g) $\frac{1}{6}$ and $\frac{1}{5}$ (h) $\frac{1}{9}$ and $\frac{1}{10}$

3 Find **three** fractions

(a) greater than one half   (b) less than one half.

4 Write a fraction

(a) smaller than one tenth   (b) greater than one third.

5 List the numbers in order.

(a) Start with the largest. $\frac{1}{2}$ $1\frac{1}{2}$ 2 $\frac{1}{4}$ $1\frac{1}{4}$ $\frac{3}{4}$

(b) Start with the smallest. $\frac{1}{3}$ 3 $1\frac{1}{6}$ $\frac{2}{3}$ $1\frac{3}{6}$ $\frac{5}{6}$

6 Copy this part of a number line:

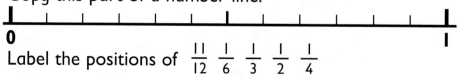

0

Label the positions of $\frac{11}{12}$ $\frac{1}{6}$ $\frac{1}{3}$ $\frac{1}{2}$ $\frac{1}{4}$

12 bears

32 penguins

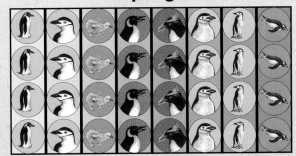

35 dogs

27 cats

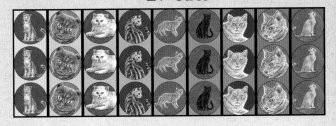

1 Find **(a)** $\frac{1}{6}$ of the bears **(b)** $\frac{1}{8}$ of the penguins

(c) $\frac{1}{7}$ of the dogs **(d)** $\frac{1}{9}$ of the cats

2 **(a)** $\frac{1}{8}$ of 72 **(b)** $\frac{1}{6}$ of 42 **(c)** $\frac{1}{9}$ of 90 **(d)** one seventh of 56

(e) $\frac{1}{6}$ of 6 **(f)** $\frac{1}{8}$ of 64 **(g)** $\frac{1}{7}$ of 21 **(h)** one ninth of 63

(i) $\frac{1}{7}$ of 63 **(j)** $\frac{1}{9}$ of 72 **(k)** $\frac{1}{6}$ of 60 **(l)** on eighth of 8

(m) $\frac{1}{5}$ of 45 **(n)** $\frac{1}{7}$ of 28 **(o)** $\frac{1}{9}$ of 54 **(p)** one sixth of 30

3

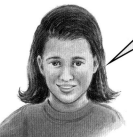

I bought six whale magnets.

Jo bought one eighth of the magnets on the whales card.

How many whale magnets were on the card?

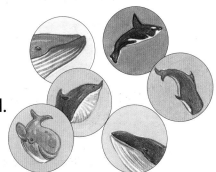

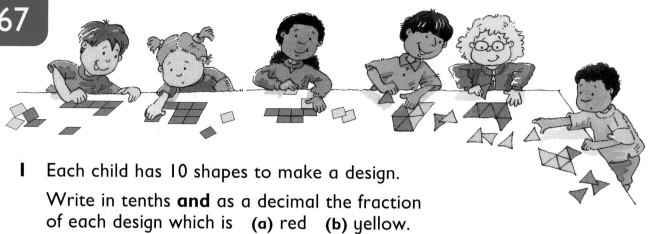

1 Each child has 10 shapes to make a design.

Write in tenths **and** as a decimal the fraction of each design which is   **(a)** red   **(b)** yellow.

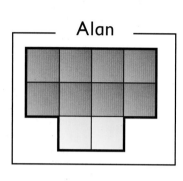

Alan

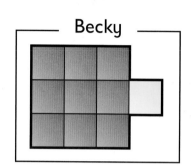

Becky

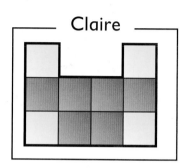

Claire

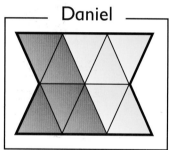

Daniel

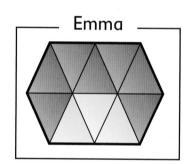

Emma

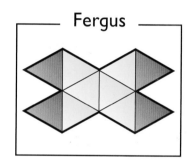

Fergus

2 Write in tenths **and** as a decimal the position shown by each arrow.

(a)

(b)
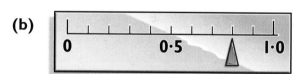

(c)
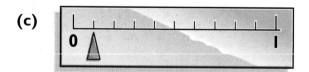

(d)
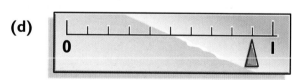

3 Write in decimal form.

(a) 7 tenths   **(b)** $\frac{1}{10}$ **(c)** 5 tenths   **(d)** $\frac{2}{10}$

1 Each **complete** tower has 10 cubes.

Jason has made $3\frac{6}{10}$ or 3·6 towers.

Write in fraction form **and** in decimal form how many towers each child has made.

Jason

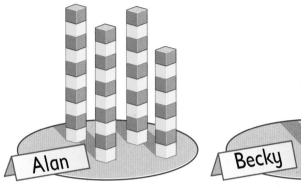

Alan

Becky

Claire

Daniel

Emma

Fergus

2 Write in fraction form **and** in decimal form the position shown by each arrow.

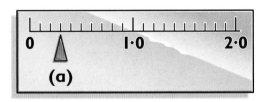

(a)

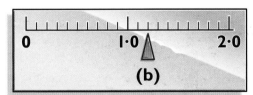

(b)

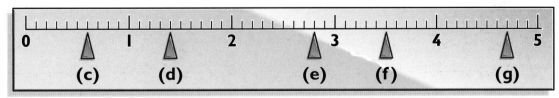

(c)   **(d)**   **(e)**   **(f)**   **(g)**

3 Write in decimal form.

(a) $\frac{9}{10}$ **(b)** five and two tenths   **(c)** $6\frac{1}{10}$ **(d)** three

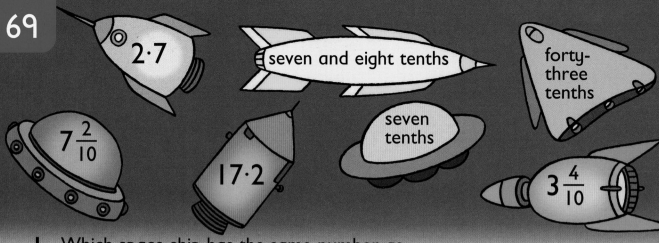

1 Which space ship has the same number as

(a) 7·8   (b) $2\frac{7}{10}$ (c) thirty-four tenths

(d) 0·7   (e) $17\frac{2}{10}$ (f) four and three tenths?

2 Copy and complete each sequence.

(a) 0·2, 0·4, 0·6, ___, ___, ___   (b) 2·6, 2·2, 1·8, ___, ___, ___

(c) 6·7, 6·4, 6·1, ___, ___, ___   (d) 2·4, 3·0, ___, 4·2, ___, ___

(e) 10·5, 10·1 ___, ___, ___, 8·5   (f) 1·4, ___, ___, 2·9, ___, 3·9

3 Write the number between:

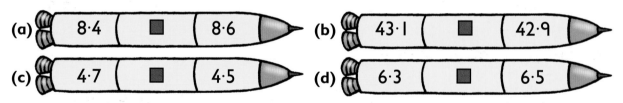

(a) 8·4 ▣ 8·6   (b) 43·1 ▣ 42·9

(c) 4·7 ▣ 4·5   (d) 6·3 ▣ 6·5

4 Write **a** number between:

(a) 3·6 ▣ 4·0   (b) 143 ▣ 143·5

(c) 9·6 ▣ 6·9   (d) 15·4 ▣ 13·0

(e) 71·4 ▣ 80   (f) 1 ▣ 2·5

1 Write the value of each **red** digit.

(a) | 1 | 3·7 |

(b) | 4 | 6·5 |

(c) | 6 | 2·2 |

(d) | 3 | 3·3 |

(e) | 5 | 8·6 |

(f) | 2 | 9·4 |

2 Write True (T) or False (F).

(a) 9·0 > 0·9   (b) 34·0 > 340   (c) 60·3 < 63·0

(d) $\frac{81}{10} > \frac{18}{10}$ (e) $4\frac{7}{10} < 7\frac{4}{10}$ (f) 9·3 < 3·9

3 Write the smallest number.

(a) 2·3   3·2   23   (b) $64\frac{1}{10}$ 64   64·6

(c) 4·1 $1\frac{1}{10}$ 1·4   (d) 155   55·1   15·5

4 List the numbers in order.
- Start with the **smallest**.

(a) 3·8   3·0   4·3   3·4   (b) 19·0   1·9   10·9   9·1

- Start with the **largest**.

(c) 2·5 $3\frac{5}{10}$ $2\frac{7}{10}$ 3·7   (d) 4·0 $\frac{4}{10}$ 14·0 $\frac{14}{10}$

5

Which space pod number is nearest to

(a) 5   (b) 3   (c) 2   (d) 6   (e) 1?

6 Round to the **nearest whole number**.

(a) 6·8   (b) 3·6   (c) 6·3   (d) 10·4   (e) 17·9

(f) 55·2   (g) 29·7   (h) 234·1   (i) 749·0   (j) 199·5

1 How many kg altogether of moonrocks did each robot pack?

(a) 0·6 kg 0·2 kg

(b) 0·3 kg 0·5 kg

(c) 0·1 kg 0·7 kg

(d) 0·3 kg 0·3 kg

(e) 0·2 kg 0·4 kg 0·3 kg

(f) 0·5 kg 0·1 kg 0·4 kg

2 Double each number.

(a) 0·4　　(b) 0·2　　(c) 0·5　　(d) 0·7　　(e) 0·9

3 (a) 0·7 + 0·3　(b) 0·6 + 0·7　(c) 0·8 + 0·9　(d) 0·5 + 0·9
　 (e) 0·7 + 0·8　(f) 0·9 + 0·6　(g) 0·6 + 0·5　(h) 0·8 + 0·4

4 Add.　(a) 0·3 + 1·5　(b) 0·6 + 4·3　(c) 0·9 + 5·1

5 Increase　(a) 2·8 by 0·5　(b) 3·9 by 0·4　(c) 1·3 by 0·8.

6  Make 1.

(a) 0·7 + ■　　　　(b) 0·1 + ■
(c) ■ + 0·5　　　　(d) ■ + 0·2
(e) 0·4 + 0·5 + ■　(f) 0·2 + ■ + 0·5

7 Find the missing numbers.

(a) ■ + ▲ = 1　　　　(b) ■ + ▲ + ◆ = 1
(c) ■ + ▲ < 1　　　　(d) ■ + ▲ + ◆ < 1

1 Find each total volume of asteroid acid.

(a)
3·5 *l* 2·2 *l*

(b)
1·6 *l* 4·3 *l*

(c)
6·5 *l* 3·4 *l*

(d)
4·1 *l* 1·7 *l*

(e)
2·4 *l* 5·3 *l*

(f)
6·2 *l* 1·8 *l*

2 Double.

(a) 2·3   (b) 1·4   (c) 4·6   (d) 3·9   (e) 2·8

3 (a) 7·7 + 1·2   (b) 5·5 + 2·5   (c) 5·8 + 2·7   (d) 3·8 + 3·4
   (e) 2·2 + 4·9   (f) 6·9 + 2·8   (g) 2·5 + 1·8   (h) 2·6 + 4·7
   (i) 7·3 + 7·9   (j) 9·7 + 4·4   (k) 5·7 + 5·7   (l) 8·6 + 6·8

Find the missing numbers.

4 (a) 2·6 + ■ = 3   (b) 4·1 + ■ = 5   (c) 5·4 + ■ = 6
   (d) ■ + 6·3 = 7   (e) ■ + 9·7 = 10   (f) ■ + 7·8 = 8

5 (a) ■ + ▲ = 6·8   (b) ■ + ▲ = 10·2   (c) ■ + ▲ = 13·5
   (d) ■ + ▲ + ◆ = 7·6   (e) ■ + ▲ + ◆ = 8·3

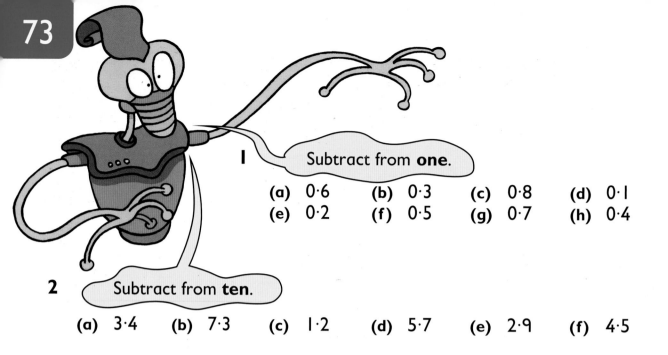

1 Subtract from **one**.

(a)	0·6	**(b)**	0·3	**(c)**	0·8	**(d)**	0·1
(e)	0·2	**(f)**	0·5	**(g)**	0·7	**(h)**	0·4

2 Subtract from **ten**.

(a) 3·4   **(b)** 7·3   **(c)** 1·2   **(d)** 5·7   **(e)** 2·9   **(f)** 4·5

3

(a)	5·6 – 0·4	**(b)**	6·7 – 0·6	**(c)**	9·9 – 1·7	**(d)**	10·8 – 5·5
(e)	7·5 – 6·2	**(f)**	8·1 – 4·0	**(g)**	6·0 – 5·0	**(h)**	3·0 – 1·9

4

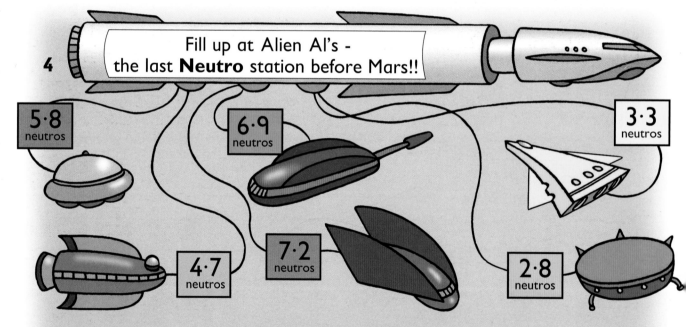

Fill up at Alien Al's - the last **Neutro** station before Mars!!

5·8 neutros

6·9 neutros

3·3 neutros

4·7 neutros

7·2 neutros

2·8 neutros

Find the difference between the fuel loads of these spaceships.

(a) blue and yellow   **(b)** orange and blue   **(c)** yellow and orange
(d) purple and green   **(e)** red and purple   **(f)** orange and green

5

(a)	7·4 – 0·6	**(b)**	10·6 – 0·9	**(c)**	5·2 – 3·5	**(d)**	6·3 – 1·4
(e)	3·1 – 1·9	**(f)**	9·2 – 5·3	**(g)**	11·5 – 9·7	**(h)**	20·4 – 19·8

1 Write the **first eight numbers** in each sequence.

(a) Start at 45.
Add 23 each time.

(b) Start at 200.
Subtract 17 each time.

(c) Start at 144.
Increase by 54 each time.

(d) Start at 86.
Add 25 each time.

(e) Start at 500.
Subtract 19 each time.

(f) Start at 849.
Decrease by 21 each time.

2 • Write the missing numbers in each sequence.
  • Describe the sequence.

(a) 210, 226, 242, 258, ■, ■, ■

(b) 175, 166, 157, 148, ■, ■, ■

(c) 152, 182, 212, 242, ■, ■, ■

(d) 601, 566, 531, 496, ■, ■, ■

3 • Which number is wrong in each sequence?
  • What should it be?

(a) 34, 48, 62, 86, 90, 104

(b) 119, 112, 105, 98, 93, 84

(c) 583, 623, 653, 703, 743, 783

(d) 547, 516, 485, 454, 423, 394

4 Start at 57. Add 21 each time.
What is the **tenth** number in the sequence?

5

The **sixth** number in my sequence is 175.
I added 25 each time.
What was my starting number?

1	2	3	4	5	6	7	8	9	10	11	12	13	14	15	16	17	18	19	20
21	22	23	24	25	26	27	28	29	30	31	32	33	34	35	36	37	38	39	40
41	42	43	44	45	46	47	48	49	50	51	52	53	54	55	56	57	58	59	60
61	62	63	64	65	66	67	68	69	70	71	72	73	74	75	76	77	78	79	80
81	82	83	84	85	86	87	88	89	90	91	92	93	94	95	96	97	98	99	100

1 Write the numbers each child can stand on.

I can only stand on multiples of 5.

Anne

I can only stand on multiples of 10.

Billy

I can only stand on multiples of 11.

Asif

I can only stand on multiples of 8.

Rosie

2 Use your answers to question 1. Which numbers are multiples of

(a) 5 and 11   (b) 11 and 8   (c) 5 and 10   (d) 5, 8 and 10?

3 On which numbers can **both** Ted **and** Saira stand?

I can only stand on multiples of 3.

Ted

I can only stand on multiples of 7.

Saira

4 Copy the Carroll diagram. Write these numbers on the diagram.

45 84 66 70 81
21 36 12 54 90

	Multiple of 6	~~Multiple of 6~~
Multiple of 9		
~~Multiple of 9~~		

5 Write True (T) or False (F).
   (a) 111 is a multiple of 11.
   (b) 102 is a multiple of 8.
   (c) 117 is a multiple of 9.
   (d) 700 is a multiple of 10 and 7.
   (e) 81 is a multiple of 7 and 9.
   (f) 96 is a multiple of 6 and 8.

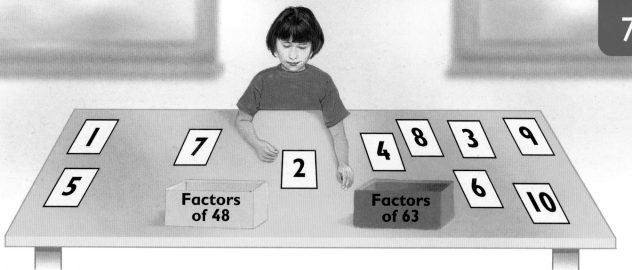

1 (a) Which number cards should Leela put in
   - the yellow box   - the green box?

 (b) Explain why some of the number cards should **not** be put in the yellow **or** green boxes.

2 Write True (T) or False (F).

(a) 20 is a factor of 100.

(b) 7 has no factors.

(c) 12 is not a factor of 50.

(d) 23 has only two factors.

(e) 15 is a factor of 30 and 50.

(f) 8 is a factor of 40 but not a factor of 100.

3 Copy the Venn diagram. Write the numbers 1 to 20 on the diagram.

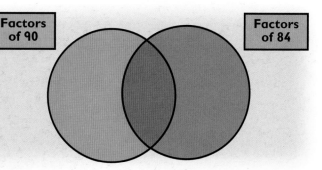

4 Use **factors** to find

(a) 8×13

(b) 6×16

(c) 17×9

(d) $72 \div 6$

(e) $126 \div 9$

(f) $120 \div 8$

Use a quarter-metre strip.

1 Measure these lengths. Label them as

| shorter than $\frac{1}{4}$ metre | **or** | longer than $\frac{1}{4}$ metre |

(a)

(b)

(c)

(d)

(e)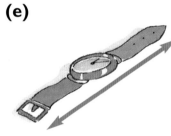

(f)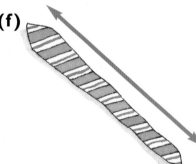

2 Find two objects
  (a) each about $\frac{1}{4}$ m long
  (b) longer than $\frac{1}{4}$ m but shorter than $\frac{1}{2}$ m.

3 Which labels show the same height?

(a)  50 cm

(b)  $\frac{1}{4}$ m

(c)  75 cm

(d)  1 m

(e)  $\frac{3}{4}$ m

(f)  100 cm

(g)  $\frac{1}{2}$ m

(h)  25 cm

The board is 1 m 90 cm wide.

1 metre 90 centimetres

1 Estimate then measure

(a) the length of two desks

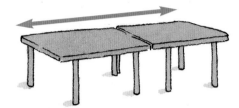

(b) your arm span

(c) the width of a bookcase

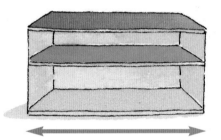

(d) the height of a door.

2 Write the missing heights.

Name	Height of sunflower		
Val	1 m 36 cm	136 cm	1·36 m
Jack	1 m 89 cm	**(a)**	1·89 m
Rosie	**(b)**	**(c)**	2·13 m
Josh	**(d)**	215 cm	**(e)**
Mo	2 m 8 cm	**(f)**	**(g)**
Kim	**(h)**	110 cm	**(i)**

3 Measure **(a)** your height **(b)** a friend's height.
Record each height in three different ways.

1 Estimate then measure each length:

  (a) the width of a window
  (b) the width of the teacher's desk
  (c) the height of the teacher
  (d) the height of your chair
  (e) the length of a gym rope
  (f) the length of a gym bench.

2 Write the length of each snake in two **other** ways.

Snake	Length of Snake		
Adder	1 m 12 cm	112 cm	1·12 m
Boa	2 m 34 cm	(a)	(b)
Anaconda	(c)	(d)	4·06 m
Cobra	(e)	328 cm	(f)
Viper	2 m 61 cm	(g)	(h)
Python	(i)	(j)	6·93 m

3 Use chalk to draw a snake

  (a) 1·25 m long
  (b) 2·38 m long.

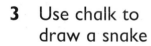

My stick is one metre long.

My stick is one metre long.

Amy

Ahmed

1 What fraction of a metre is each coloured part of Ahmed's stick?

2 Use a metre stick or a tape marked in tenths of a metre.
Measure objects like these to the **nearest tenth of a metre**.

3 Alan jumped $2\frac{7}{10}$ m or **2·7 m.**

Write the length of each of these jumps in another way.

	Jade	David	Anna	Li	Stuart
Length of jump	$2\frac{4}{10}$ m	(b)	$3\frac{1}{10}$ m	(d)	$4\frac{5}{10}$ m
	(a)	3·6 m	(c)	2·9 m	(e)

4 Measure the length of your own jump to the nearest tenth of a metre.

5 Write in order.

(a) Start with the shortest.

123 cm	1 m 28 cm	1·2 m	$1\frac{1}{4}$ m	$1\frac{3}{10}$ m

(b) Start with the longest.

$3\frac{3}{4}$ m	3·8 m	372 cm	$3\frac{1}{2}$ m	$3\frac{7}{10}$ m

1 Who has given the best answer?

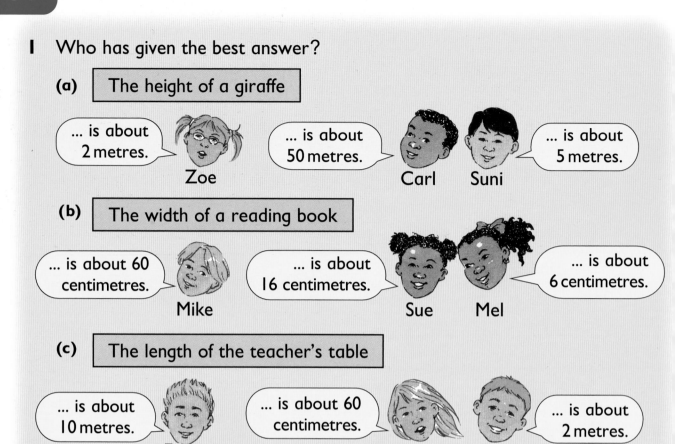

(a) | The height of a giraffe

... is about 2 metres.
Zoe

... is about 50 metres.
Carl   Suni

... is about 5 metres.

(b) | The width of a reading book

... is about 60 centimetres.
Mike

... is about 16 centimetres.
Sue   Mel

... is about 6 centimetres.

(c) | The length of the teacher's table

... is about 10 metres.
Ewan

... is about 60 centimetres.
Jess   Pete

... is about 2 metres.

2 Which of these

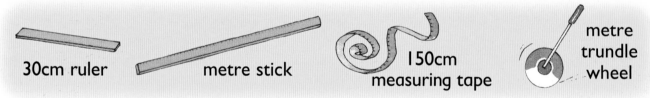

30cm ruler   metre stick   150cm measuring tape   metre trundle wheel

would you use to measure

(a) your height   (b) the length of a screw

(c) the length of the school hall

(d) the length of a pencil

(e) the distance around a basketball

(f) the width of a football pitch

(g) the distance around a tree trunk?

3 List four other things you would measure in

(a) centimetres   (b) metres.

1 **(a)** Mark out a square of side 25 metres.

(b) Find how long you take to walk around its perimeter.

(c) Estimate how long you would take to walk **1 kilometre.**

2 Write in metres.

(a) 2 km   **(b)** 5 km   **(c)** $3\frac{1}{2}$ km   **(d)** $\frac{3}{10}$ km

(e) 4 km 300 m   **(f)** $2\frac{1}{10}$ km   **(g)** 3 km 230 m   **(h)** $1\frac{1}{4}$ km

(i) $1\frac{8}{10}$ km   **(j)** 1 km 507 m   **(k)** $\frac{9}{10}$ km   **(l)** 5 km 342 m

3 Write in kilometres and metres.

(a) 2168 m   **(b)** 1820 m   **(c)** 3004 m   **(d)** 7060 m

4 Write in kilometres.

(a) 7000 m   **(b)** 5000 m   **(c)** 2500 m   **(d)** 8700 m

5

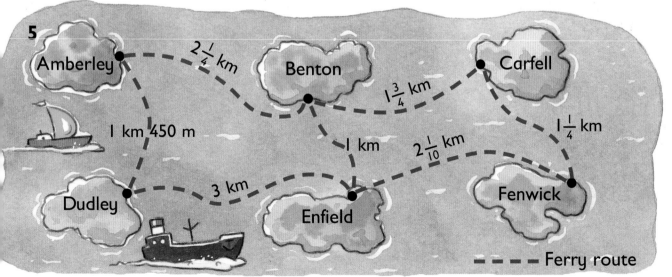

Write in metres the **shortest** distance between

(a) Amberley and Enfield   **(b)** Benton and Fenwick

(c) Dudley and Carfell   **(d)** Amberley and Fenwick.

1   Which items weigh

(a) more than $\frac{1}{2}$ kg

(b) less than $\frac{1}{2}$ kg

(c) less than $\frac{1}{4}$ kg

(d) more than $\frac{3}{4}$ kg

(e) more than $\frac{1}{2}$ kg and less than $\frac{3}{4}$ kg

(f) more than $\frac{1}{4}$ kg and less than $\frac{1}{2}$ kg

(g) between $\frac{3}{4}$ kg and 1 kg?

2   List **two** items which together weigh

(a) $\frac{3}{4}$ kg

(b) $1\frac{1}{4}$ kg

(c) $1\frac{1}{2}$ kg

(d) 1 kg?

3   List **three** items which together weigh $1\frac{1}{2}$ kg?

4   How many more grams should be added to make

(a) $\frac{1}{2}$ kg

(b) $\frac{1}{4}$ kg

(c) $\frac{3}{4}$ kg

(d) 1 kg?

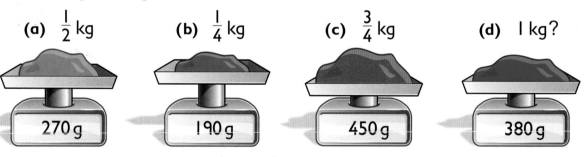

5   Write in order, starting with the lightest weight.

| 550 g | $\frac{1}{4}$ kg | $\frac{3}{4}$ kg | 200 g | $\frac{1}{2}$ kg | 1000 g | 700 g |

1 Use  .

How many

(a) pencils altogether weigh about 50 g

(b) exercise books altogether weigh about 200 g?

2 Find something that weighs between 150 g and 250 g.

3 The box weighs less than 800 g.

Write about the weight of each of these items.

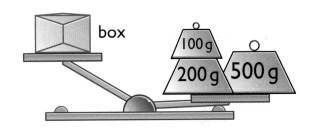

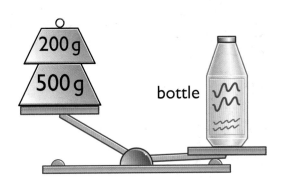

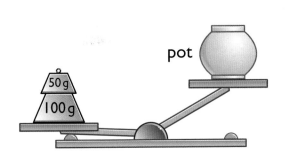

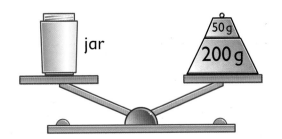

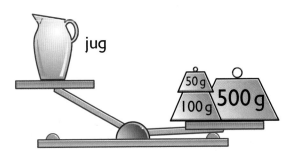

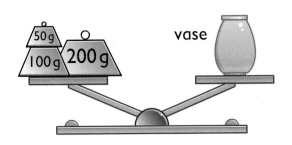

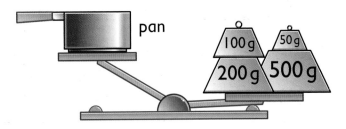

1 Beth has some 500 g, 200 g, 100 g and 50 g weights.

List the weights she could use to balance each item.

Use as few weights as possible.

(a)

(b)

(c)

(d)

2 Find the weight of

(a) the box

(b) the tin

(c) the bottle

(d) the jar.

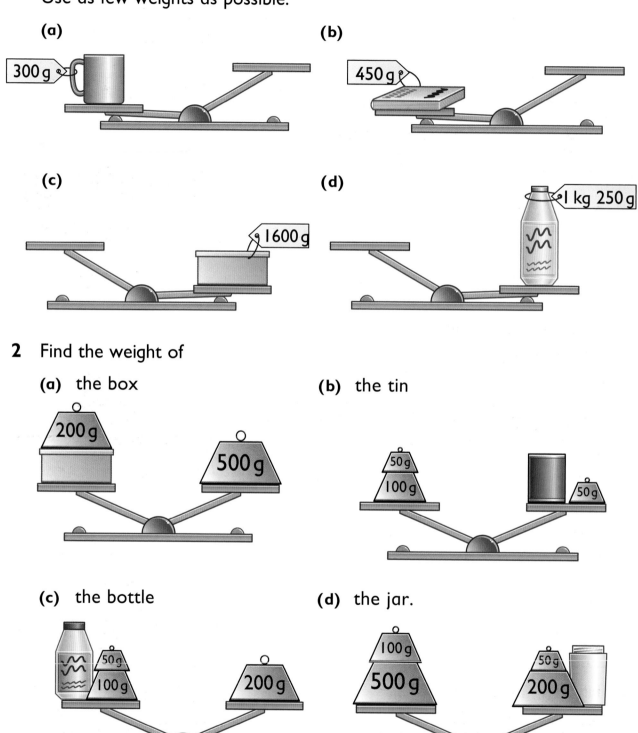

1 Write the weight of each item **to the nearest 100 g.**

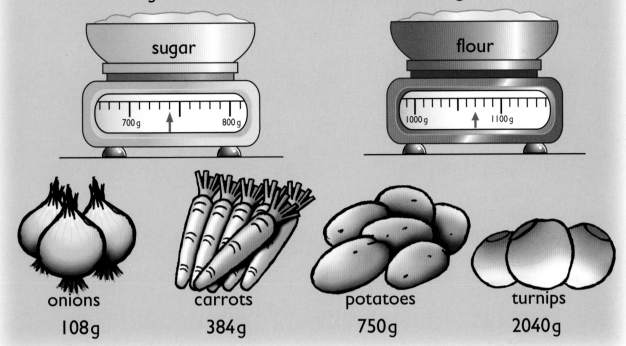

sugar   700 g   800 g

flour   1000 g   1100 g

onions	carrots	potatoes	turnips
108 g	384 g	750 g	2040 g

2 Find the approximate weight of each bag.

A   B   C   D   E

3 Make up bags with these weights.

   F   about 600 g

   G   about 400 g

   H   about 250 g

4 Find an object which weighs

   (a) less than 100 g

   (b) between 650 g and 850 g

   (c) about 1 kg 200 g.

1 Write in order

(a) starting with the **lightest** weight

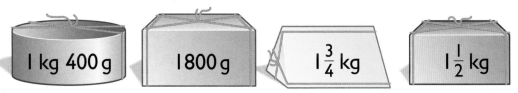

1 kg 400 g   1800 g $1\frac{3}{4}$ kg $1\frac{1}{2}$ kg

(b) starting with the **heaviest** weight.

1300 g $1\frac{1}{4}$ kg   1500 g   1 kg 200 g

2 Write in **grams**.

(a) 1 kg 650 g   **(b)** 3 kg 485 g   **(c)** 2 kg 193 g   **(d)** 2 kg 95 g

3 Write in **kilograms and grams**.

(a) 2222 g   **(b)** 1906 g   **(c)** 1100 g   **(d)** 3070 g

4 Write the total weight in **kg and g** of the tins on each tray.

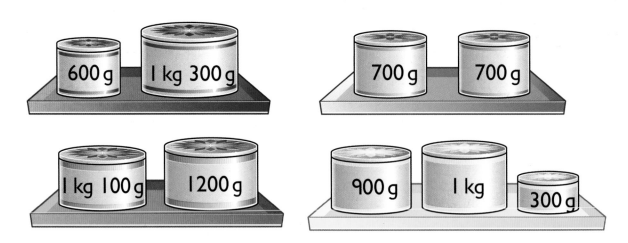

600 g   1 kg 300 g   700 g   700 g

1 kg 100 g   1200 g   900 g   1 kg   300 g

5 Which trays have tins which together weigh

(a) more than $1\frac{3}{4}$ kg   **(b)** less than 2000 g?

1 Write in grams.

(a) $2\frac{3}{4}$ kg   (b) $1\frac{7}{10}$ kg   (c) $3\frac{3}{10}$ kg   (d) $4\frac{1}{10}$ kg

(e) 1 kg 210 g   (f) 3 kg 250 g   (g) 1 kg 75 g   (h) 2 kg 200 g

2 Write in kilograms and grams.

(a) $3\frac{1}{2}$ kg   (b) $2\frac{1}{4}$ kg   (c) $6\frac{6}{10}$ kg   (d) $5\frac{4}{10}$ kg

(e) 3510 g   (f) 2050 g   (g) 1718 g   (h) 4605 g

3 Write the weights in order.

(a) Start with the heaviest.

 1274 g    $1\frac{8}{10}$ kg $1\frac{1}{4}$ kg    1kg 650g

(b) Start with the lightest.

 1 kg 50 g    $\frac{9}{10}$ kg   1210 kg    0·5 kg

4 Write each new weight in kg and g.

(a) Add 400 g.

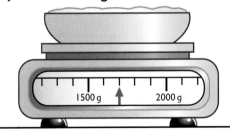

(b) Remove 300 g.

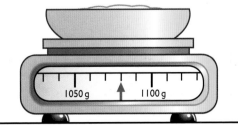

(c) Double the weight.

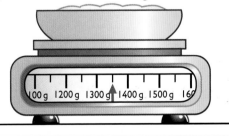

(d) Halve the weight.

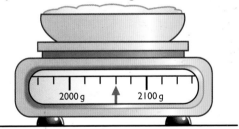

Use water or sand, a and a  1 litre $\frac{1}{2}$ litre

1 You need containers like these.

Find to the nearest half-litre the amount of sand or water each container holds.

LEMON 250 ml
APPLE 750 ml
STRAWBERRY 900 ml
PEAR 800 ml
PEACH 400 ml
PLUM 200 ml
ORANGE 600 ml
GRAPE 500 ml

2 Which juice containers hold

(a) more than $\frac{1}{2}\ell$ (b) less than $\frac{1}{2}\ell$ (c) less than $\frac{1}{4}\ell$

(d) more than $\frac{3}{4}\ell$ (e) between $\frac{1}{4}\ell$ and $\frac{3}{4}\ell$

(f) more than $\frac{1}{2}\ell$ and less than $\frac{3}{4}\ell$?

3 List **two** containers which together hold

(a) 1ℓ (b) $\frac{3}{4}\ell$ (c) $1\frac{1}{4}\ell$ (d) $1\frac{1}{2}\ell$.

4 List **three** containers which together hold $1\frac{1}{4}$ litres.

5 Write in order, starting with the smallest amount.

$\frac{3}{4}\ell$	1001 ml	$\frac{1}{2}\ell$	300 ml	$\frac{1}{4}\ell$	850 ml	1ℓ

1 Write each missing amount from the table.

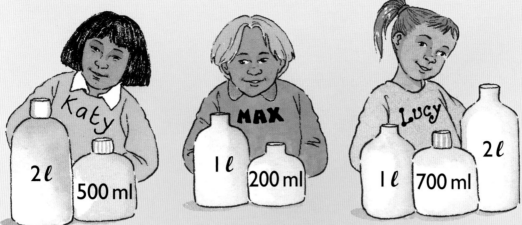

Name	Amount	
Katy	2ℓ 500 ml	2500 ml
Max	1ℓ 200 ml	(a)
Lucy	(b)	3700 ml
Colin	(c)	(d)
Mia	(e)	(f)

2 Write in millilitres.

(a) 2ℓ 450 ml (b) 1ℓ 710 ml (c) 3ℓ 805 ml (d) 1ℓ 25 ml

3 Write in litres and millilitres.

(a) 1760 ml (b) 3333 ml (c) 4308 ml (d) 2050 ml

4

How many of each container can be filled from the 1 litre barrel?

Use centimetre cubes.

1 **(a)** Make these pieces from the puzzle.
Find the volume of each in cubic centimetres.

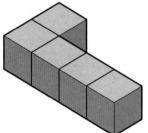   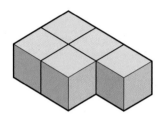   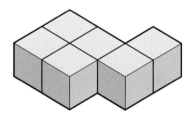

(b) Put the three pieces together to make a cuboid and find its volume.

2 Repeat question **1** for these pieces.

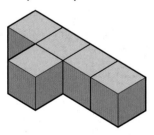   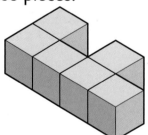   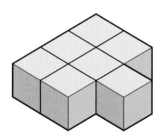

3 Find the volume in cm^3 of each of these pieces.

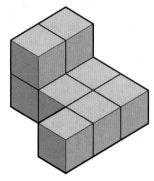   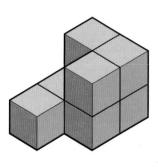   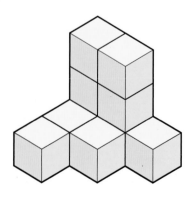

Use centimetre cubes.

1   For each shape find
   (a)   the volume in cubic centimetres
   (b)   the least number of cubes needed to make it a cuboid
   (c)   the volume of the **cuboid**.

2   Check by building each cuboid.

(a)

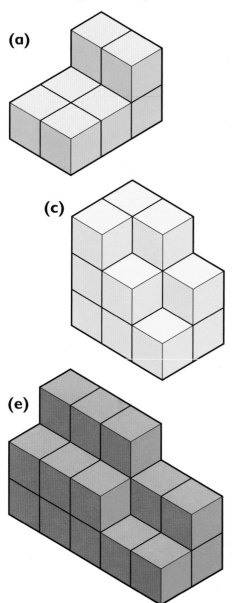

(b)

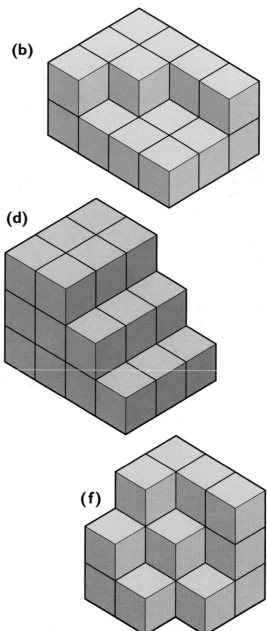

(c)

(d)

(e)

(f)

3   Make as many different cuboids as you can,
    each with a volume of 20 cm³.

1 Find the area of each rectangle in cm².

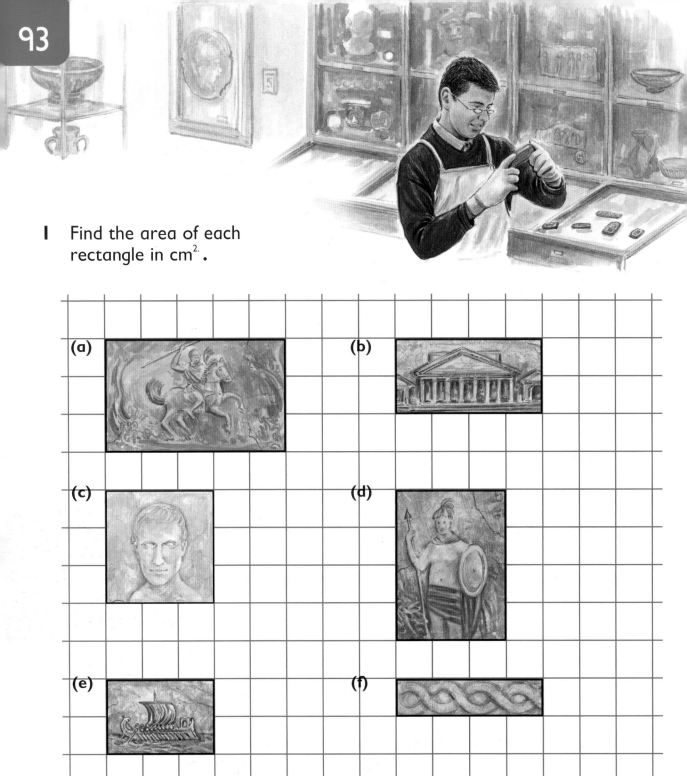

(a)

(b)

(c)

(d)

(e)

(f)

(g)

2 Draw 2 different rectangles each with an area of 20 cm².

Work as a group.
You need metre sticks, large sheets of paper and sticky tape.

Megan and Ethan have
square Roman mosaic tiles.

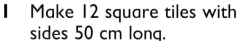

1   Make 12 square tiles with
    sides 50 cm long.

2   **(a)** Join 4 tiles together to make a
        larger square like this:

    (b) What is the length of each
        side of the large square?

    (c) What is the approximate area
        of your square?

> **The square has an area of about 1 square metre, 1 m².**

3   **(a)** Lay 4 tiles together to make each of these shapes.

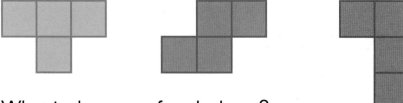

    (b) What is the area of each shape?

    (c) Make two different shapes each with an area of 2 m².

1 (a) This jug has 365 ml of milk in it. How much will be left after I pour out 180 ml?

(b) This rope is 5 metres long. What length is left when I cut off 65cm?

(c) My dog weighs 18 kilograms. My brother is two and a half times as heavy. What is his weight?

(d) The capacity of the bucket is 5 litres. The cup holds one quarter of a litre. How many cupfuls of water are needed to fill the bucket?

2 Sarah needs four lemons to make 400 ml of lemonade. What volume of lemonade can she make with twelve lemons?

3 List the ingredients for 24 of these cakes.

Ingredients for 6 cakes

100g	flour
80g	butter
50g	sugar
2	eggs

4 How many pieces of string, each 40 cm long, can be cut from a 3 m length?

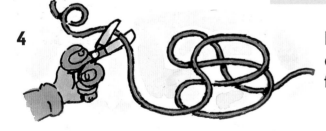

5 Sandra buys 20 litres of orange juice for a party. How many **glasses** of orange can she pour if each glass holds 200 millilitres?

1 Write these times.

(a)  **(b)**  **(c)**

(d)  **(e)**  **(f)**

(g) quarter to 6 **(h)** 12 minutes past 9 **(i)** 18 minutes to 2

2  ⟶ 26 minutes to 7.

Write these times.

(a)  **(b)**  **(c)**

(d)  **(e)**  **(f)**

3 Write these times in order.

(a) Start with the latest time.

(b) Start with the earliest time.

1 Write the time

(a) 50 minutes **after**

(b) 65 minutes after

(c) 1 hour and 30 minutes after

(d) 45 minutes after

(e) 70 minutes after

(f) 1 hour and 40 minutes after

(g) 55 minutes **before**

(h) 85 minutes before

(i) 1 hour and 50 minutes before

(j) 45 minutes before

(k) 95 minutes before

(l) 1 hour and 55 minutes before

2 How many minutes are there between each Start and Finish time?

| Start | Finish | | Start | Finish |

(a)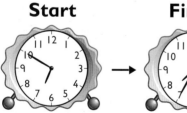

(b)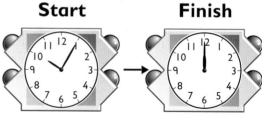

(c)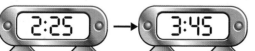

(d)

1 The Jacksons left Mandalay Bay at 7.15am. The journey to Pyramid Lake took 1 hour and 20 minutes. At what time did they arrive?

2 They arrived at French Towers at 10.10am. The journey took 90 minutes. When did they leave Pyramid Lake?

3 (a) They left French Towers at noon. How long did they stay?

(b) The journey to Wild West City took 115 minutes.

At what time did they arrive?

4

Buses to Cowboy Creek leave every 20 minutes from 8.10am.

What is the **earliest** time the Jacksons could have caught a bus to Cowboy Creek?

5 (a) The train from Wild West City to Fantasy Castle left 95 minutes late at 7.50pm. When should it have left?

(b) The Jacksons arrived in Fantasy Castle at 9.30pm.

How long was their journey?

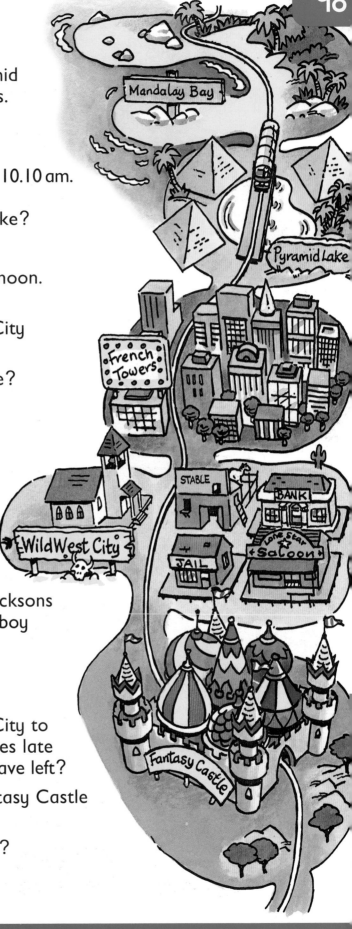

1 Write the time

(a) 17 minutes after

(b) 23 minutes after

8:17

(c) 36 minutes after

(d) 8 minutes before

2:51

(e) 24 minutes before

(f) 42 minutes before

10:46

2 How many minutes are there between each of these times?

(a)

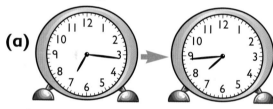

(b)

1:02   1:53

3 Hannah started a puzzle at 3.13pm. She took 38 minutes to complete it.

At what time did she finish?

4 Yani took 47 minutes to complete a jigsaw. He finished at 9.58 am.

When did he start?

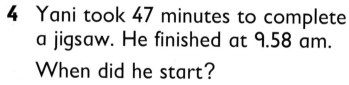

5 Eric and Petra started playing at 12.11 pm and finished at 12.50 pm.

For how long did they play?

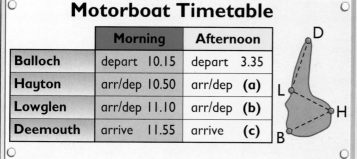

Motorboat Timetable

	Morning	Afternoon
Balloch	depart 10.15	depart 3.35
Hayton	arr/dep 10.50	arr/dep **(a)**
Lowglen	arr/dep 11.10	arr/dep **(b)**
Deemouth	arrive 11.55	arrive **(c)**

1 How long does the motorboat take to sail

   (a) from Balloch to Hayton   **(b)** from Hayton to Lowglen

   (c) from Lowglen to Deemouth   **(d)** from Balloch to Deemouth?

2 At what time should the **afternoon** boat arrive at

   (a) Hayton   **(b)** Lowglen   **(c)** Deemouth?

3

Car Ferry to Benbray

Departs: 7.30 am 10.00 am
12.30 pm 3.00 pm 5.30 pm

Sailing time: 25 minutes

How much time is there

   (a) between ferries to Benbray

   (b) between the first and last ferry?

4 What is the arrival time in Benbray of the ferry which

   (a) departs at 10.00 am   **(b)** departs at 5.30 pm?

5 How long does each person have to wait for a ferry?

   (a) Alana – arrives at 11.35 am   **(b)** Jason – arrives at 4.05 pm

6 The 12.30 pm ferry departs 40 minutes late.

   (a) At what time does it depart?

   (b) When does it arrive at Benbray?

Work with a partner.

You need cubes and a timer.

1 Find out how many times in **one minute** you can

  (a) write your name

  (b) touch your toes.

2 (a) How long do you **think** you would take to count out 100 cubes?

  (b) Use the timer to find out.

3 Which length of time is most likely to be correct?

  (a) Frying an egg takes ...

 ... about three minutes.   ... about thirty minutes. ... about an hour.

  (b) You sleep at night for ...

... about five hours. ... about fifteen hours. ... about ten hours.

  (c) Walking across the playground takes ...

 ... about two seconds. ... about twenty seconds. ... about one hundred and twenty seconds.

4

Summer lasts for three **months**.

Suggest something you would measure in

  (a) minutes **(b)** seconds **(c)** hours

  (d) weeks **(e)** days **(f)** years.

5 For how many months have you lived? Explain your answer.

1 Which diagrams show **parallel** lines?

(a) (b) (c) (d)

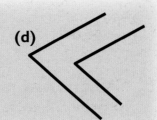

2 Which diagrams show **perpendicular** lines?

(a) (b) (c) (d)

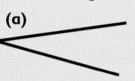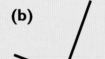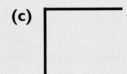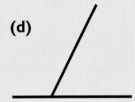

3 Which shapes have

(a) parallel lines and **no** perpendicular lines
(b) perpendicular lines and no parallel lines
(c) parallel lines **and** perpendicular lines
(d) neither parallel lines nor perpendicular lines?

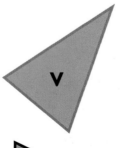

R   S   T

U   V   W

X   Y   Z

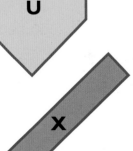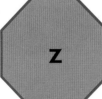

1 Which of the shapes is Zoë describing?

All the angles are right angles.
The opposite sides are equal **and** parallel.

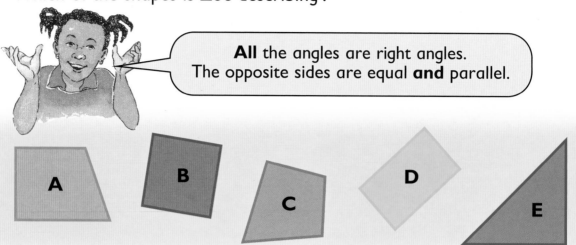

2 Name the shapes
   (a) with more than two diagonals
   (b) with **only** two right angles
   (c) with opposite sides that are equal **and** parallel
   (d) that are irregular.

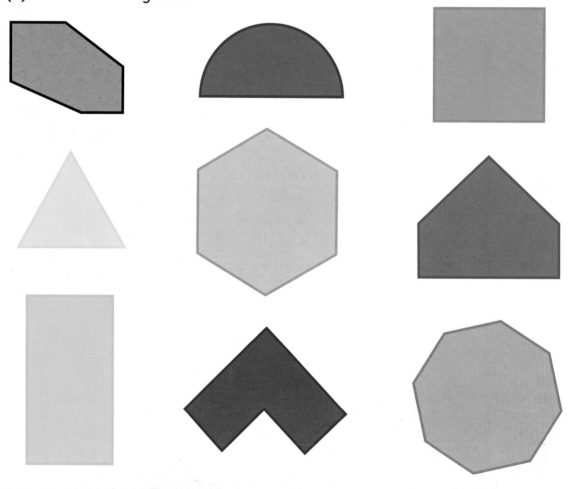

Brad: All of the sides are of equal length.

Jenny: Only two angles are equal.

1 Who is describing

(a) an isosceles triangle

(b) an equilateral triangle?

2 Which of these shapes are
- equilateral triangles
- isosceles triangles?

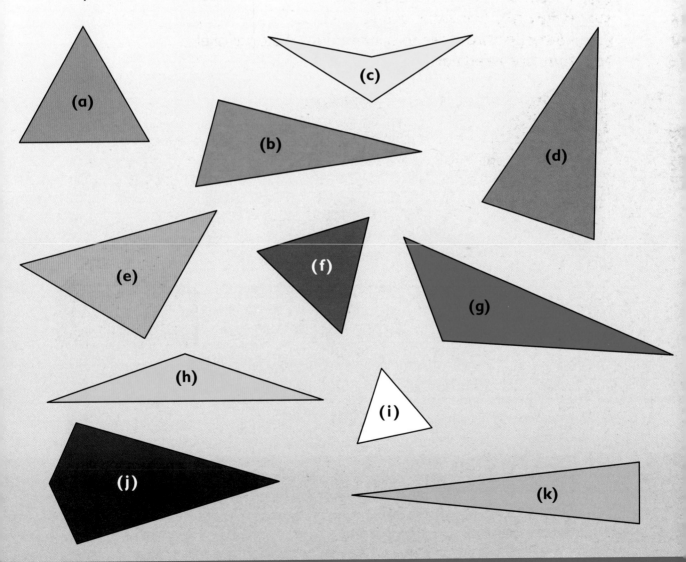

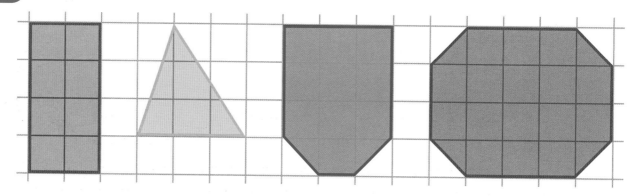

1 (a) Copy each shape on squared paper.
   (b) Draw all the lines of symmetry.
   (c) Write the total number of lines of symmetry on each shape.
   (d) Cut out the shapes and stick them in your exercise book.

2 Name the shapes which have

   (a) only one line of symmetry   (b) no lines of symmetry
   (c) more than one line of symmetry.

3 (a) Use the Shapes sheet.
        Repeat questions 1 (b), (c) and (d) for each shape.

   (b) Copy and complete a table like this:

Shape	Number of equal sides	Number of equal angles	Number of lines of summetry
Equilateral triangle	3	3	

   What do you notice?

Quasim makes tiled floor designs.

1 (a) Copy each floor design on squared paper.

(b) Colour the designs so that each has two lines of symmetry.

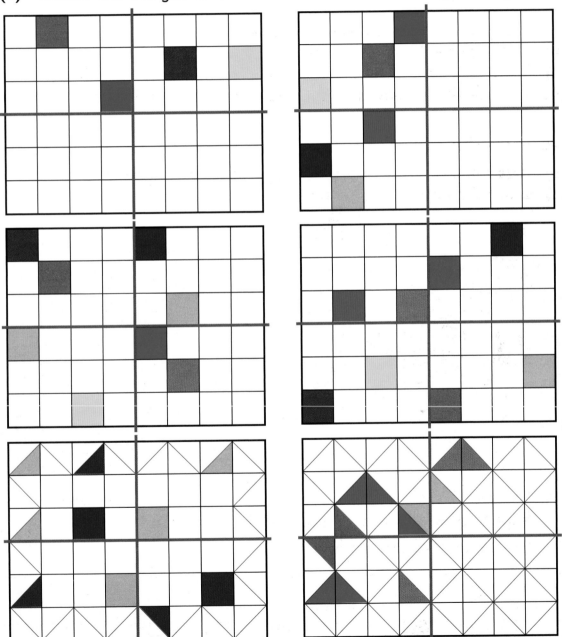

2 Draw and colour your own floor design.

1 Use a set of identical shapes in two colours to make each tiling.

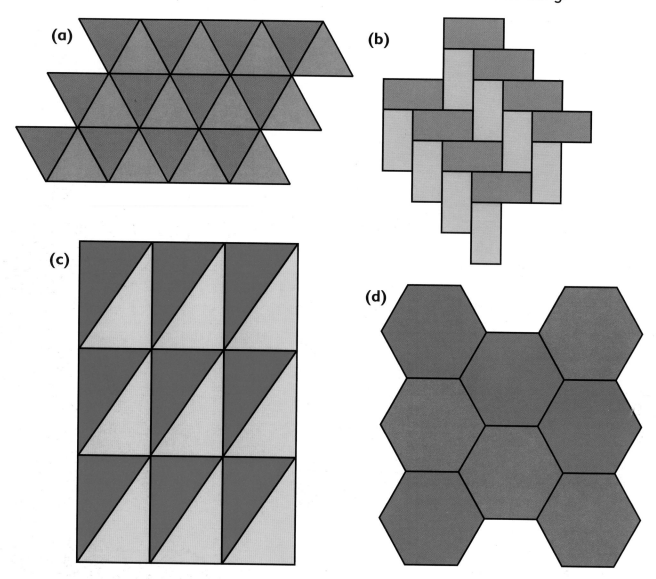

(a)

(b)

(c)

(d)

2 (a) Try to make tiling using ● regular pentagons ● regular octagons.
(b) What do you notice each time?

3 Use sets of identical shapes like these.
Investigate ways of fitting the shapes together to make tilings.

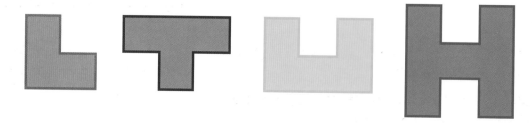

Work in pairs. Use the sheet of tiles.

1 **(a)** Cut out the tiles.

(b) Fit the tiles together to make these two different patterns.

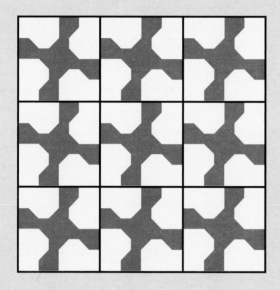 

(c) Make a different pattern with your tiles.

(d) Choose the pattern you like best and stick the tiles on a large sheet of paper.

2 **(a)** Make tiles like this on squared paper.

(b) Cut out the tiles.

(c) Fit them together to make patterns.

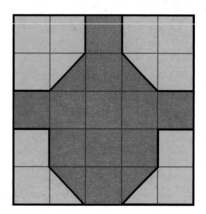

3 Design your own tiles on squared paper. Make patterns with them.

Stick the tiles on a large sheet of paper to make the pattern you like best.

1 Draw and colour circle patterns like these.

2 **(a)** Fold and cut coloured circles. Make patterns like these.

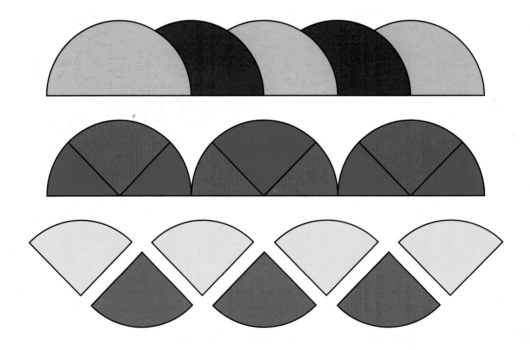

(b) Make circle patterns of your own.

You need 3D shapes like these.

1 Write the name of each shape. Choose from the labels.

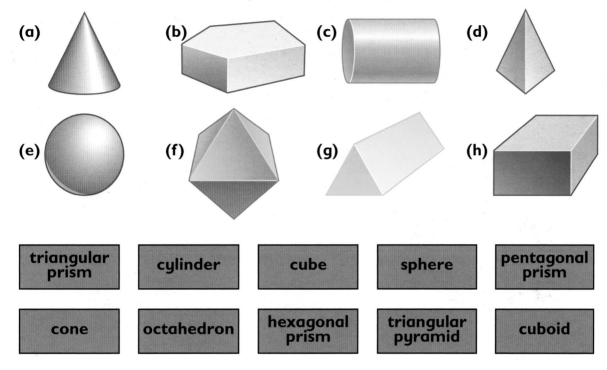

(a)　(b)　(c)　(d)

(e)　(f)　(g)　(h)

triangular prism	cylinder	cube	sphere	pentagonal prism

cone	octahedron	hexagonal prism	triangular pyramid	cuboid

2 Which shape could be in the bag? Name **two** shapes each time.

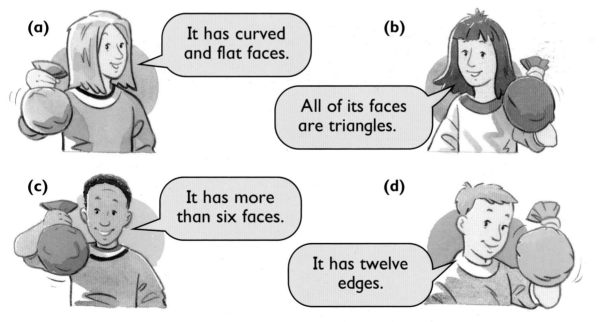

(a) It has curved and flat faces.

(b) All of its faces are triangles.

(c) It has more than six faces.

(d) It has twelve edges.

3 Write a clue to describe each of these shapes.

(a) 　(b) 　(c)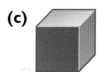

1   List the co-ordinates of
    ● the vertices of each half shape
    ● the vertices needed to complete each shape so that
      the **red** line is an axis of symmetry.

(a)

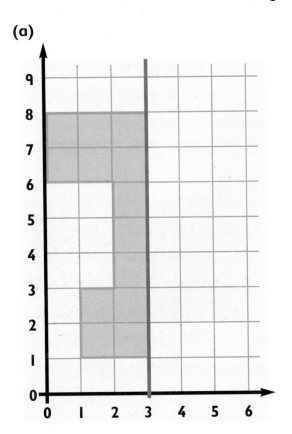

(b)

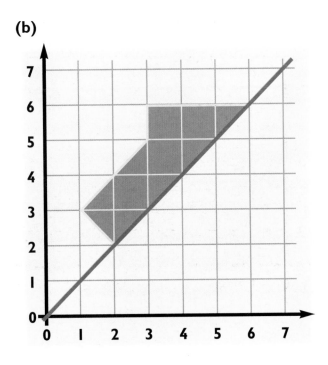

(c)

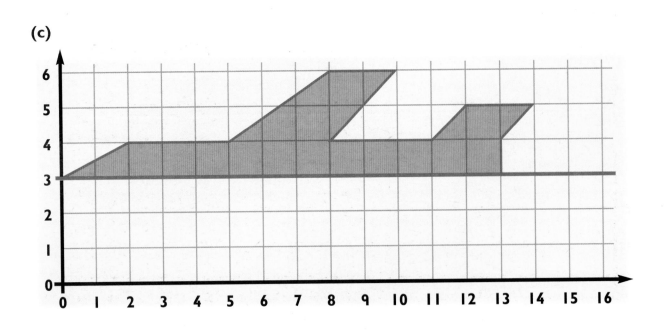

1 Write the co-ordinates of the **vertex** needed to complete each shape.

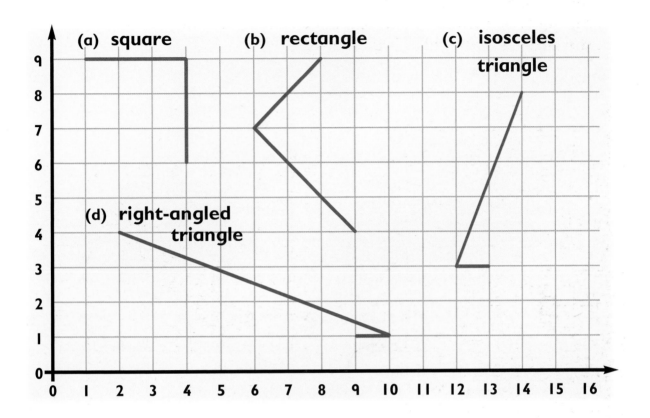

(a) square (b) rectangle (c) isosceles triangle

(d) right-angled triangle

2 Write the co-ordinates of the **end points** of a line of equal length **and** parallel to

(a) the red line (b) the black line (c) the green line.

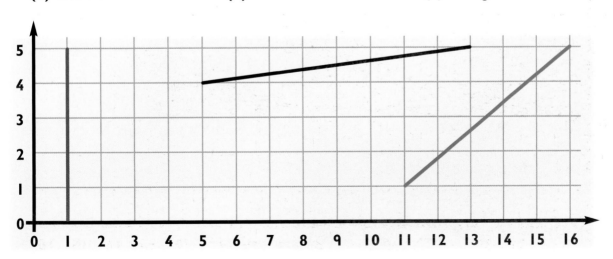

1 **(a)** Copy the shape on squared paper.

(b) Sketch the shape to show its position after it has moved
2 units to the right.

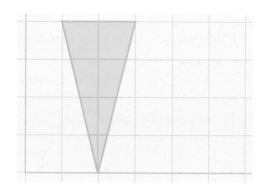

2 Repeat question **1** for these shapes and movements.

(a) **2 units to the left**

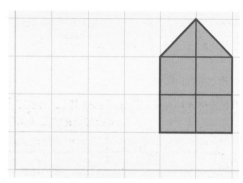

(b) **3 units to the right**

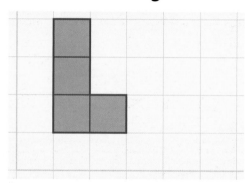

(c) **4 units to the right**

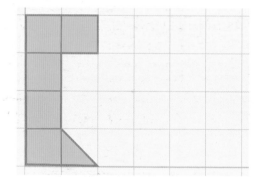

(d) **3 units to the left**

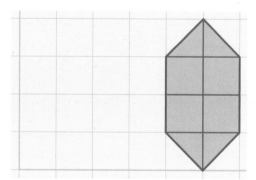

3 Translate the shape **4 units to the right**. Repeat until the strip is filled.

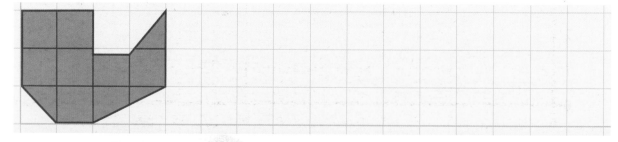

1 List the co-ordinates of the vertices of each shape
- in the position shown
- after the shape has moved

(a) two units right   **(b)** three units left

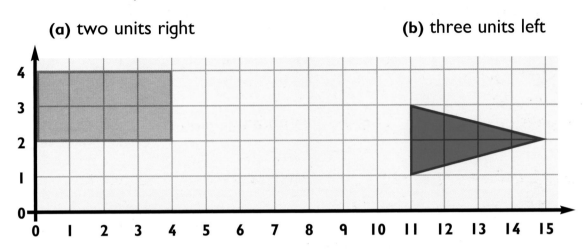

(c) one unit up   **(d)** three units down   **(e)** one unit right **and** two units up

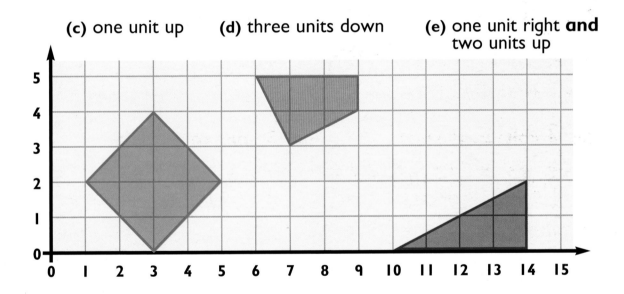

(f) six units left **and** two units down.

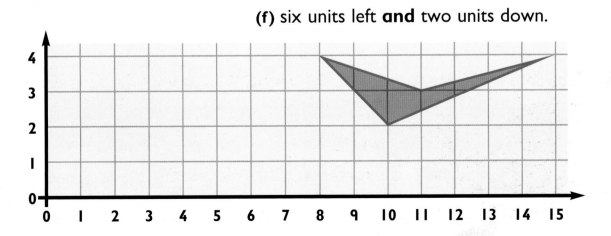

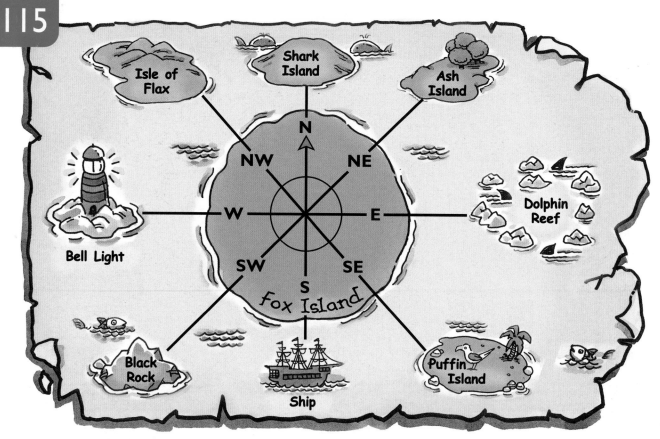

You are at the centre of Fox Island.

1 **Face North.**
In which direction are you facing after you turn through

(a) 90° anti-clockwise   **(b)** 180° clockwise

(c) 45° clockwise   **(d)** 360° anti-clockwise?

2 **Face South-east.**
What do you see after you turn through

(a) 90° clockwise   **(b)** 45° anti-clockwise

(c) 180° anti-clockwise   **(d)** 45° clockwise?

3 Describe each turn.

(a) Face Puffin Island. Turn to face Ash Island.

(b) Face Black Rock. Turn to face Bell Light.

(c) Face Isle of Flax. Turn to face Puffin Island.

(d) Face Ash Island. Turn to face Shark Island.

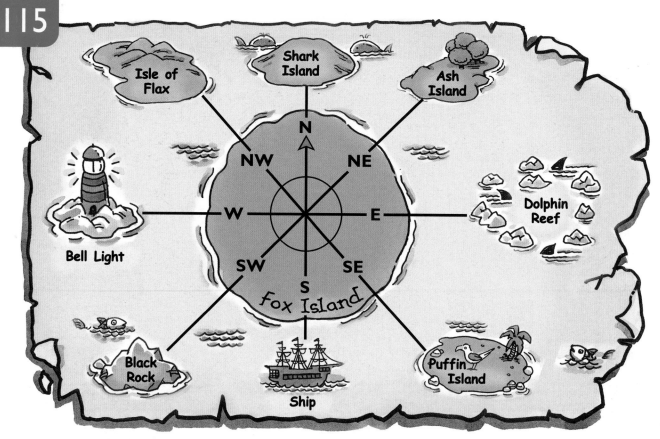

1 Through how many degrees does the pointer turn when it moves

(a) clockwise from *off* to *cold*
(b) anti-clockwise from *hot* to *warm*
(c) clockwise from *very hot* to *cool*
(d) clockwise from *cold* to *warm*
(e) anti-clockwise from *very cold* to *very hot*
(f) clockwise from *warm* to *cool*?

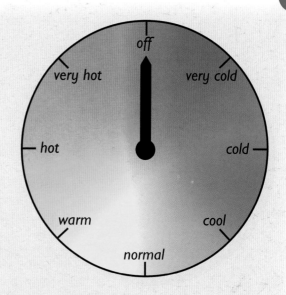

2 Which setting is the pointer facing after it turns

(a) 45° clockwise from *normal*
(b) 135° anti-clockwise from *off*
(c) 360° anti-clockwise from *hot*
(d) 270° clockwise from *cold*?

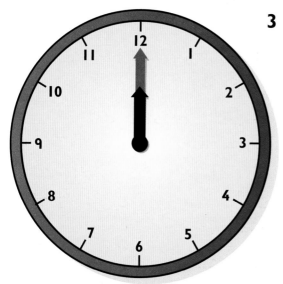

3 Through how many degrees **clockwise** does the **hour** hand turn when it moves from

(a) 12 o'clock to 3 o'clock
(b) 4 o'clock to 5 o'clock
(c) 8 o'clock to 10 o'clock
(d) 7 o'clock to 1 o'clock
(e) 6 o'clock to 3 o'clock
(f) 5 o'clock to 9 o'clock
(g) 9 o'clock to 2 o'clock
(h) 1 o'clock to 11 o'clock?

4 What time does the clock show when the hour hand moves clockwise

(a) 60° from 5 o'clock
(b) 180° from 10 o'clock
(c) 270° from 12 o'clock
(d) 330° from 11 o'clock?

The numeral **4** can be written
using the commands:

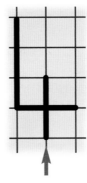

FD 2	BK 1	RT 90	FD 1

BK 2	LT 90	FD 3

1   Write commands for each of these numerals.
Start with the position and direction shown each time.

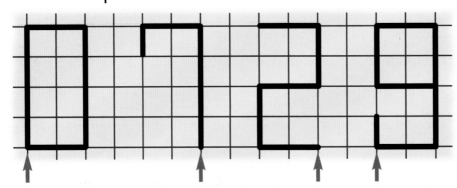

Use squared paper.

2   Follow these commands to write other numerals.
Start facing this way ↑ each time.

(a)

RT 90	FD 2	LT 90	FD 2	LT 90	FD 2
BK 2	RT 90	FD 2	LT 90	FD 2	

(b)

RT 90	FD 2	LT 90	FD 2	LT 90	FD 2
RT 90	FD 2	RT 90	FD 2		

(c)

FD 2	BK 2	RT 90	FD 2	LT 90	FD 2
LT 90	FD 2	RT 90	FD 2	RT 90	FD 2
RT 90	FD 1				

3   Write commands to draw the numeral **8**.
Do **not**
  - use the command **BK**
  - go over the same line more than once.

Draw an arrow to show where you started.

1 **(a)** Which angles are
- right   • acute   • obtuse?

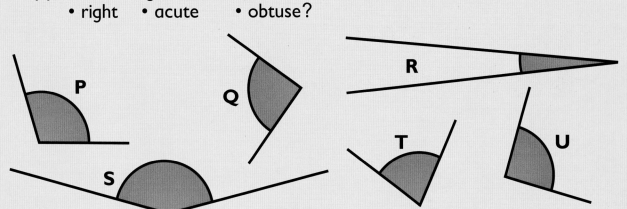

(b) List the angles in order, starting with the smallest.

2 Which shape has

(a) only two acute and only two obtuse angles

(b) two right angles, one acute angle and one obtuse angle

(c) **all** of its angles obtuse

(d) **none** of its angles obtuse

(e) only two acute angles and only one obtuse angle

(f) three obtuse angles and one acute angle

(g) one right angle, two acute angles and one obtuse angle?

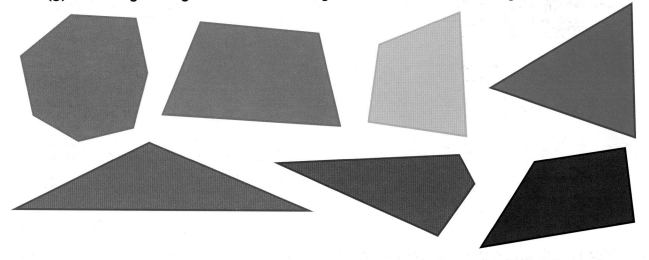

3 Draw a **quadrilateral** which has two **opposite** acute angles
and two **opposite** obtuse angles.

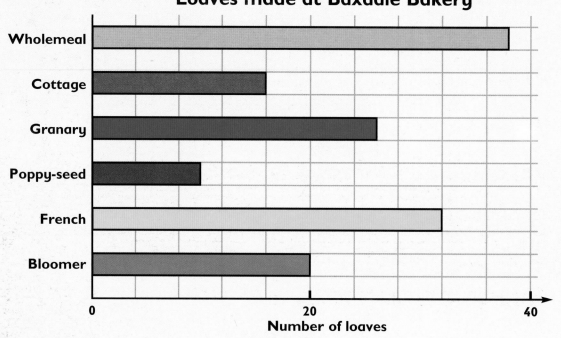

Loaves made at Baxdale Bakery

Number of loaves

1 Which kind of loaf did the bakery make
   (a) most of   **(b)** least of?

2 How many of each kind of loaf were made?

3 How many **fewer** Cottage loaves were made than
   (a) French   **(b)** Granary   **(c)** Wholemeal?

4 The bakery made scones for Baxdale School Fayre.
   Draw a **bar chart** to show the information
   in the table.

Scones baked

Plain	Fruit	Cherry	Treacle	Bran	Cheese
20	34	14	30	8	28

Drinks bought at Baxdale School Fayre

Number of drinks

coffee	tea	mineral water	orange juice	hot chocolate

1 Which drink was the most popular?

2 How many of each type of drink were bought?

3 How many drinks were bought altogether?

4 (a) Which drink was twice as popular as mineral water?
(b) Suggest a reason for this.

5 Draw a **bar line chart** to show the information in the table.

Number of visitors in the café at

10.15	10.30	10.45	11.00	11.15	11.30
20	62	54	46	28	12

1 The table has information about special breads from Baxdale Bakery.

Number of loaves baked		Colour	Shape	Flour	Finish
Adrian	12	white	round	plain	seeds
Lisa	18	white	twisted	plain	nuts
Bindu	16	brown	round	wholemeal	seeds and nuts
Pamela	24	white	stick	plain	seeds and nuts
Jo	10	brown	twisted	granary	nuts
Scott	20	white	round	plain	seeds

(a) How many loaves were baked altogether?

(b) Who is correct and who is wrong? Explain.

Less than half of the loaves are finished with seeds **or** nuts.

Anna

About one quarter of the loaves are brown.

Jason

2 In which ways are Adrian's and Bindu's loaves

(a) the same   (b) different?

3 Name each baker.

(a)  I made twice as many loaves as Jo.

(b)  My loaves are sticks.

(c)  I made brown twisted loaves.

(d)  The flour in my twisted loaves, finished with nuts, is **not** granary.

About half of the boys in our school have 4 or 5 letters in their first name.

Class 5 carries out a survey to find out if what their teacher says is true.

Baxdale School - Letters in boys' names

3	Ⅲ Ⅲ	
4	Ⅲ ⅢⅢ ⅢⅢ ⅢⅢ	
5	ⅢⅢ ⅢⅢ ⅢⅢ ⅢⅢ ⅢⅢ ⅢⅢ Ⅱ	
6	ⅢⅢ ⅢⅢ ⅢⅢ ⅢⅢ ⅢⅢ ⅢⅢ	
7	ⅢⅢ ⅢⅢ	

1 **(a)** How many boys' names have

- 3 letters   • 4 letters   • 5 letters
- 6 letters   • 7 letters?

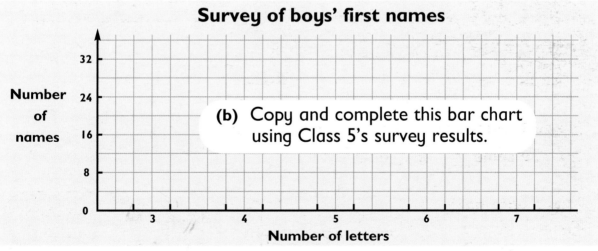

Survey of boys' first names

Number of names

32
24
16
8
0

(b) Copy and complete this bar chart using Class 5's survey results.

3   4   5   6   7

Number of letters

2 **(a)** How many boys' names altogether are in the survey?
 (b) Which number of letters in a name is the **mode**?
 (c) What **fraction** of the names have 6 letters?

3 **(a)** Write the greatest and the smallest number of letters in a name.
 (b) What is the **range**?

4 Is it true that about half of the boys' names have 4 **or** 5 letters? Explain.

1 Jonjo the clown has these choices of make-up:

wigs	curly	straight	bald
noses	circle	triangle	square
mouths	happy	sad	normal

List all the different faces Jonjo can have.

2

Sander's Circus

1 show each day Mon – Fri

2 shows each day Sat and Sun

- Jonjo appears in 6 shows each week.
- He only works on 4 days.
- Only 2 of his working days are consecutive.

On which days of the week does Jonjo work?